REVIVING BUILDINGS
AND COMMUNITIES

REVIVING BUILDINGS AND COMMUNITIES

a manual of renewal

MICHAEL TALBOT

Line illustrations by Michael Clark

DAVID & CHARLES

Newton Abbot   London   North Pomfret (Vt)

British Library Cataloguing in Publication Data

Talbot, Michael, *1934–*
  Reviving buildings and communities: a manual of renewal
  1. Historic buildings — Great Britain — Conservation
  and restoration
  I. Title
  363.6′9′0941   NA109.G7

ISBN 0-7153-8679-4

Typeset by ABM Typographics Limited, Hull
and printed in Great Britain
by Redwood Burn Limited, Trowbridge, Wilts.
for David & Charles Publishers plc
Brunel House   Newton Abbot   Devon

Published in the United States of America
by David & Charles Inc
North Pomfret   Vermont 05053   USA

CONTENTS

'I have always loved above all others what I call Cinderella country. I know of nothing more exciting to my imagination than discovering in the wasteland, which the established world rejects as ugly and sterile, a beauty and promise of rare increase not held out anywhere else in life'

Laurens van der Post, *The Heart of the Hunter*

'There was nothing special about the places concerned, there were no secret resources to be drawn upon — people simply used their imagination, commissioned good architects and designers, and got on with it'

Lionel Esher, *The Continuing Heritage*

PREFACE
AND ACKNOWLEDGEMENTS

There are a number of technical books about old buildings and how to save them and there are numerous travellers' guides and more weighty volumes that describe their history and architecture. Wisely or not, this one aims to combine some of the elements of both and add perhaps a little of the excitement of an adventure story. From the viewpoint of the organisers as much as the architects and builders, it attempts to tell the story of a number of projects that have succeeded in rescuing run-down buildings from the brink of final decay, and in one case starting the rescue of a whole town. Often the work has been done against all the odds; that is to say the omens for success were no more favourable, often less so, than for similar work in most places. Yet done it was, sometimes through the spontaneous will of small local voluntary groups, sometimes by larger organisations at a regional or national level, sometimes by local authorities, always with enthusiasm and imagination.

It also sets out some of the tools of the trade, organisations, funding, regulations, some of the inherent advantages and disadvantages of the alternative methodology and where to seek advice. In this way it gives an indication of what has been proven beyond doubt to be practicable and, hopefully, how to set about achieving it.

The projects were chosen on the basis of geography to give a reasonable spread across the country, of building types, of illustrating the range of organisations behind them and of the widely different contexts — small towns, inner cities and rural — in which the buildings stand. Others, equally successful, could have been chosen and would have been if the objective had been a comprehensive catalogue. The ones that are included may possibly serve to whet the appetite for more of the same, particularly in the towns and areas where the need is greatest.

About half the material is based on an unpublished RIBA report on revolving funds that I prepared in 1982–3 on a part-time basis when employed by Suffolk Coastal District Council. For this initial impetus thanks are due to the RIBA for placing their confidence in untried hands, to the many individuals and organisations that contributed information, advice and encouragement, and to the council for what proved to be an absorbing semi-sabbatical. The report completed, possibilities for publication were considered. A positive response from David & Charles led to the report being almost completely rewritten and considerably enlarged.

Many people have helped, among them some very much at the coalface in the charitable trusts, like Mrs Dorothy Brown (Bristol), Douglas Blain (Spitalfields), Mrs Dorna Daw (Bradford-on-Avon), Oliver Barratt (Cockburn) and Alan Simpson (Northern Heritage Trust). Neal Sharp of the National Trust for Scotland was always among the first to respond to requests for information. For the local authorities, Miss Kate Dawkins provided useful background material about Bristol, and Peter Richards helped with Essex; the Rt Hon Francis Pym MC, MP, generously gave time to discussing Hazells Hall; Michael Middleton and Miss Rosemary Watt of the Civic Trust were consistently encouraging and helpful; Miss Sophie Andreae of SAVE Britain's Heritage contended with a string of questions about country houses. Kit Martin took the trouble to read through and comment on parts of the draft, and so did architects Jim Read (English Heritage), David Bagshaw, Derek Latham and Gordon Michell. Michael Thompson of Lloyds Bank, Nicholas Falk of the Urban and Economic Development Group (URBED), Anthony Foord of the Suffolk Historic Churches Trust and many other trusts and individuals were also most helpful at draft stage. None of this makes them in any way responsible for any errors or omissions, for the opinions expressed or for the conclusions reached but, in a small way, the help of so many people may reflect the team effort that is vital to the revival of places and communities.

Finally mention should be made of the patience with which my wife, Rosalind, deciphered the hand-written manuscript into typed form and coped with second thoughts.

Part I
PROJECTS – THE BACKGROUND

The phenomenal growth of the conservation effort in recent years is shown vividly in the expansion of the Civic Trust's Architectural Heritage Fund, which, on a revolving basis, provides short-term loans to buildings preservation trusts and other charitable bodies. Starting from scratch with a capital of £1 million on 26 May 1976, the fund was fully committed within four years, revolved at full stretch for the next three, needed an extra £½ million in 1983 to keep up with demand, followed by a similar amount barely two years later. The winter 1984/5 newsletter for buildings preservation trusts, 'Preservation in Action' reported that 'the Fund's basic capital, in consequence, will shortly stand at about £2 million. Ten years ago this would have seemed almost too good to be true; today it is abundantly clear that it is not enough.'

The reason it is not enough is that the scope for imaginative and yet practical renovation, transforming apparently redundant eyesores into properties that are both usable and ornamental, seems boundless. It is an almost limitless opportunity that only becomes a burden if it is disregarded. The projects illustrate the transformation and represent a range of situations and buildings that are mirrored in numerous places where properties, in spite of conservation's headway, still stand neglected.

Memories can be short. The improvements that have resulted from these and similar projects soon become part of the everyday scene and are quickly taken for granted — in a way that is a measure of their success. But only a short time ago, when the battles of the Euston Arch, the Coal Exchange, of many country houses and of numerous less celebrated properties were being fought and lost, projects like these would have been considered utopian. In some places, no doubt, they would be still. It should serve as a tribute and inspiration to recall and record a little of what has been done.

1
TOWN AND COUNTRY

Bradford-on-Avon, Wiltshire

Whereas the silk weavers in late seventeenth-century Spitalfields brought prosperity to that area of London for little more than fifty years, the cloth weavers in Bradford-on-Avon sustained a stable community for several centuries. From the tenth century onwards, Bradford-on-Avon thrived on the manufacture of cloth so the present town, largely untouched by Victorian industrialisation and redevelopment, has inherited a legacy of good buildings from many periods. It has also inherited a sense of civic pride which, as far as its buildings are concerned, is embodied in the Bradford-on-Avon Preservation Society, founded in 1959 when there was a great deal of run-down property in the town and a general move towards demolishing it. Ten years later the society, wishing to do more than comment or criticise, joined forces with a sister organisation established in 1964, the Bradford-on-Avon Preservation Trust, pooling its resources of 180 members with the latter's financial assets of over £3,000 and charitable status. This amalgamation brought into being the Preservation Trust of today.

Before this combination of forces, a move towards restoring old buildings at risk had been made in 1966 when a founder member and later chairman, Elizabeth Stephenson, presented the trust with a fifteenth-century barn, known as the Priory Barn. With support from the preservation society, the trust set about converting it into a small hall combining the twin benefits of a headquarters for itself and a new social facility for the town as a whole. From the hall's opening in 1969 it became well used for all sorts of occasions, and the trust established itself as a key element of the Bradford-on-Avon community. Part of the same building was later converted into a dwelling-house, incorporating a seventeenth-century plaster ceiling from a derelict house in Frome, Somerset.

With the proceeds from the sale of another property given by a trust member, the neglected, mainly Georgian, Silver Street House was purchased for restoration in 1975. The house had been used as a pub and hotel for many years; the main staircase had been removed and the

originally well-proportioned rooms much altered, but several beauti-
fully panelled rooms remained (one was earmarked as the trust's registered office), and the imposing façade was of classical proportions and
important to the curve of the street. Except for the office, the property
was converted back into residential use as one maisonette and four
small flats[1] and leases offered for sale. After sales were completed, the
trust helped to set up a management company representing the
leaseholders which would be responsible for the corporate maintenance
of the property. The work was completed in 1979 and the trust recovered
its original capital.

Admirable though the Priory Barn and Silver Street schemes were in
their own right, they had an equally valuable purpose in enabling the
trust to limber up for its next, far more daunting, exercise, 5–8 Market
Street. The momentum gained by these successes was timely, for when
the trust acquired the Market Street properties in August 1980, their
condition was so critical that they were thought unlikely to survive
another winter. Market Street is one of the main arteries in Bradford-
on-Avon and Nos 5–8 had been described by a senior DoE inspector as
'one of the most charming minor essays' in the town. Since its construction in the late eighteenth or early nineteenth century, when Market
Street was called Pippet Street, the terrace had been in use by various
small shopkeepers and their families. As recently as the 1960s, the
shops were still quite flourishing, accommodating a clockmaker, a
greengrocer, a fish shop and, at No 8, a pet shop, though by then the
upper floors were largely uninhabited. But within a few years, except
for the clockmaker, they had fallen vacant.[2] Lacking routine maintenance, the terrace gradually fell into disrepair. Around 1972, by then
totally unused and in a serious state, they were purchased by a property
developer whose contribution to conservation was to gut the two inner
units, stripping out even the floors and floor joists. This aggressive act
and the ensuing local protests persuaded the local authority, West
Wiltshire District Council, to serve a repairs notice, only to withdraw
it when it was realised that should the owner fail to carry out the work
specified in the notice the council might then be obliged to proceed with
compulsory purchase of the property and bear the cost of its renovation;
at the time it seemed that little, if any, grant aid for this could be
expected from the DoE.

Since the council seemed unwilling to take effective action, the trust
commissioned an architect's costed sketch scheme for the renovation of
the terrace, followed in September 1977 by a more detailed feasibility
study involving engineers and quantity surveyors. Grant aid was inves-

12

tigated, the Bradford Town Council discussed launching a public appeal for funds to restore the shops and the district council considered compulsory purchase on behalf of the trust. At that juncture a private property developer working on another restoration project in the town expressed an interest in carrying out the trust's scheme and financial help was offered by the latter in the shape of a low-interest loan towards the cost of purchase. Before this could be implemented, a third developer appeared and in July 1979 acquired the property, but only with the apparent intention of allowing it to deteriorate beyond recall, since a further nine months elapsed without progress on repairs. Visitors to the town, having seen the eyesore in Market Street, would reproach the trust, which was mindful of the costs involved and up to 1979 already committed in Silver Street, for apparently doing nothing.

Things came to a head in May 1980 following more local lobbying and press coverage, and the trust was offered the property for £20,000, presenting it with a momentous choice between proceeding with the purchase, renovation and the probable expenditure of £200,000 (nearly three times the cost of the Silver Street scheme) or standing aside with the virtual certainty that the buildings would be lost. After much deliberation the trust decided to offer £18,000, which was accepted provided contracts were exchanged within fourteen days. The money for purchase was found, the district council contributing £2,000, scaffolding was erected and emergency repairs instigated to protect passers-by from falling debris. Work began in earnest in August 1981, the money coming from a variety of sources, including generous grant aid from the Historic Buildings Council and two grant-making trust loans of £5,000 each.

Two features of the fund raising are particularly noteworthy: approaches to local bank managers, apparently failing to spot the public relations potential of the scheme, met with no success, but a National Westminster branch in Bath agreed a substantial loan at a commercial rate of interest on condition that it was given the trust's account — shopping around rewarded. The second feature, as outstanding as the renovation itself, was the remarkable success of the trust in raising money through social and charitable occasions. Having already established itself socially at Priory Barn, the trust was able to organise a series of events, from bicycle rides and cake-making to poetry and musical evenings, which in two years raised over £13,000. The most lucrative events were a fifty/fifty auction (£1,660), a sponsored walk (£1,000), a nearly-new sale (£999), the fund-raising launching party (£978), the monthly market stall (£911 over two years) and the sponsored bicycle rides (£631). The proceeds from many others were in three figures. In all there were about fifty individual events over the two years, averaging one every other week which must have involved nearly everyone of active age in the town (see section on 'Local fund raising' in Chapter 10 for a complete list of events). The scheme at 5–8 Market Street thus became a cause for the town's 8,000 population as well as for the trust.

In only ten months the transformation of the terrace from eyesore to showpiece was complete, the original upper-level dwellings reinstated as self-contained maisonettes and the shops available to serve local residents and visitors once again. At first glance, the refurbished and freshly named Pippet Buildings have a straightforward, repetitive look, particularly the main façade. Closer inspection reveals a subtle variation of detail, a reflection of the minor alterations that had been made over the years as a consequence of repair and changing occupants and use. The trust and its architects took the view that these individual lighter touches, as in the shop fronts, gave character and interest without challenging the integrity of the terrace as a whole and so were worth keeping. The effect is charming. Two members of the trust's Council of Management undertook to act as estate agents, all the shops and maisonettes were reserved a month before the end of the contract and the final balance sheet showed a 12 per cent net profit on the total capital cost. The thoughts of the local bank managers who, in the early stages, refused to assist the scheme are not recorded.

In July 1982, to round off the Market Street story in appropriate style, the late writer and broadcaster Alec Clifton-Taylor came to Bradford-on-Avon to officially open the scheme. On the two following Saturdays it was open to the public. Behind this fairy-tale ending there lies the formidable combination of effort, practical know-how, imagination and ability on the part of the trust and its advisers. The officers of the trust were, and still are, a mixed blend, then consisting of a school teacher, potter, chartered accountant, research biochemist and, as president, Dr Alex Moulton of bicycle fame. United by a common enthusiasm for conservation, they saw to it that the potential of a thoroughly run-down old property, in other places too often unregarded, was appreciated by and exploited for the people of Bradford-on-Avon who, one way or another, all took part and the whole town reaped the benefit.

Essex

In contrast to Suffolk's Coastal's three schemes (see p 30) comprising a total of twenty-eight properties, the pattern of Essex County Council's revolving fund is of a larger number of smaller schemes, eight comprising fourteen properties to date. The difference shows how market pressures can change quite sharply even over relatively short distances. The demand for residential property in both Essex and Suffolk is strongly influenced by the accessibility to London of the place concerned, along with local factors such as the availability of alternative accommodation, the appeal of an individual property and the area, and ease of access to workplaces. Most of Essex is within commuter range of London and the parts of the county nearest to the capital are protected by Green Belt status, limiting the provision of housing in the area of greatest demand. Recognising development pressures to come, about one third of the county, most of it now Green Belt, was included in the London Metropolitan Region boundary in the Ministry of Housing & Local Government's 1964 South-East Study, an historic government report on the problems likely to arise as a result of population growth in the twenty years up to 1981.

The result in the Green Belt has been strong demand, pushing up prices and making worthwhile the renovation of anything remotely capable of repair and conversion. As long as planning control sees that the work is carried out in a suitable manner — unfortunately not always easy as much of it lies outside the normal control powers of the planning authorities — market pressures should ensure that buildings are usually well and — with luck — sympathetically cared for. For ten or fifteen miles beyond the Green Belt, market pressures have a similar effect, but in the outer fringes of Essex that belong more to the East Anglian region than London region, thirty-five to seventy miles from the capital, the County Council has found individual historic buildings badly in need of repair, sometimes having been on the market for several years. On the Suffolk coast, eighty or more miles from London with demand reduced accordingly, the problem was whole groups as well as individual derelict buildings. The conservation programmes adopted by the Essex and Suffolk local authorities were a reflection of the very different opportunities and needs of their areas.

It was in 1972 that Essex County Council formed a team of officers from its Estates, Architects, Finance and Planning departments to present the council with proposals on a revolving basis for the acquisition, repair and sale of historic buildings needing attention in conservation areas. For this purpose, the council had obtained an interest-free loan

15

from the Pilgrim Trust[1] of £10,000 which it decided should be topped up as necessary, also interest-free, from the council's capital reserves. Its only other source of finance has been Historic Buildings Council grants. In comparison with Suffolk Coastal District Council's revolving fund, the Essex version has the great advantage of being completely interest-free, reducing the apparent cost of the building work and avoiding the catastrophic effect of slow sales, resulting in crippling interest charges over an extended period.

Of the eight Essex schemes, five have made profits and three losses. It achieved a valuable confidence-building early success by making just over £3,000 on a scheme for the repair of three cottages in East Street, Coggeshall, costing £20,000 inclusive of fees to architects and selling agents. The next two schemes, in Manningtree and Witham, made losses and for a few months the fund was marginally in the red but it recovered with two single-house projects in Bocking and Halstead, the latter recording an impressive 50 per cent surplus on the total cost. At the end of 1979, after five projects, the running balance stood at almost £20,000, all clear profit to the council; a tangible reward, along with the lasting improvements in the five towns, for a degree of imagination, skill and risk not shown at the time by anyone in that area in the private sector.

Though considerably smaller, the county council's next project, in Harwich, had much in common with Suffolk Coastal's scheme at Leiston, undertaken at a similar financial highpoint. Unbeknown to the two local authorities, the Leiston and Harwich schemes started within a few months of each other. In Harwich, the run-down of the docks has led to the closing of cafés, pubs and tourist-based shops and a decline in the town's economic activity. At the unfashionable end of Essex, furthest from London than anywhere in the county, Harwich offers relatively low prices to the house purchaser, but with its balance sheet firmly in the black, the council decided that the renovation of 30 West Street was a worthwhile risk. When, after about two years of unsuccessful marketing, the property was eventually resold, the balance sheet recorded a loss of £4,500, about 10 per cent of the purchase and restoration cost. At a time of exceptionally high interest rates, the loss would have been more than double if interest charges had been included, but the county council's example seems to have inspired at least one enterprising private renovate-and-sell business. Betty Holbrook may only be a one-woman conservation team but since she started setting her own example in 1979 she has completed and sold about half a dozen listed properties in the Harwich conservation area and has plans for more. She reduces her costs by employing direct labour and joining in with the building

16

work herself. Building renovation, to her, is a productive hobby which she expects to pay for itself with a bit in hand. Mrs Holbrook's are among about twenty projects in the town that have followed the council's in West Street.

In the conversion of a weather-boarded eighteenth-century vicarage coach-house, a minor accent in a street described by Alec Clifton-Taylor as one of the prettiest in England, the less chilling climate of photogenic Thaxted restored the fund to profitable ways with an approximately 16 per cent return on the capital cost. The most recent project in the series, the medieval Guildhall at Clavering close to the Hertfordshire border, was once the property of the Society for the Protection of Ancient Buildings and is protected by National Trust covenants. At one time five tenements, the council scheme has produced two houses and promises to provide another useful surplus.

Over the years the county team, unchanged throughout, has developed sufficient confidence, understanding and collective experience that it can now work quickly, by shorthand rather than longhand. Properties have been purchased on the open market without recourse to compulsory powers, in all cases after the property had failed over a period of several months to find a private buyer. The design work is carried out by the county architect's department, whose fees are charged to the scheme. The distance of the schemes from County Hall in Chelmsford, makes it impractical for the council to handle sales enquiries so local estate agents are appointed to sell the properties. In what is seen as a recognition of market demand, coloured bathroom suites are included as standard. All the properties have been sold freehold. If leasehold disposals were deemed necessary, the council would wish to transfer the freehold to a third party so as to clear the project off the council's books entirely.

The Essex experience is that sale prices usually turn out to be better than expected. The publicity generated by the schemes has been beneficial for council public relations and has consolidated support within the council: when members have been invited to site visits they have shown considerable interest. Although the revolving fund is not budgeted separately from other council activities, it can be readily identified to show how the profits and losses are working out. Since the scheme is funded, in the main, on the basis of loans, the revolving fund is in effect the running balance or profits. Without HBC and Civic Trust grants, all of them coming under the heading of works within conservation areas, the fund would have recorded losses on all projects with the exception of 36–38 Head Street, Halstead.

17

The county team believes that the cost of renovation has always been less than the cost of an equivalent new building. In most cases, a suitable replacement building would have been uneconomic and it is likely that either an empty site or a cheap and inappropriate replacement would have resulted if the existing property had been demolished. In the case of 36–38 Head Street, Halstead, where a suitable new building might have been economic, the team believes that modern regulations would have prevented redevelopment because of the particularly restricted nature of the site.

So far, the directly council-sponsored method of renovation has worked well in Essex. The work has been of a consistently high standard and the turnover of schemes has been steady. The possibility of forming a county building preservation trust is considered from time to time but the council-run method, with its experienced team, is straightforward and proven. From the team's ability to call on interest-free loans, it follows that one of the main reasons for a trust — cheap capital — has no attraction, and a trust's repair bills would probably be higher because of the burden of VAT, which is reclaimed by the council. The general uncertainty about VAT and its application has further discouraged changes that might produce less favourable financial circumstances than those already enjoyed by the council's team. Grants from the Historic Buildings Council (now English Heritage) have supported every project. The HBC grants policy of making the most effective use of a limited budget by concentrating on towns which have an established conservation scheme would, in normal circumstances, have led to refusals of grant, but the revolving fund itself was accepted as meeting the requirements of a scheme. The fund has therefore enabled help to be given to projects that would otherwise have been ineligible for grant assistance.

Perhaps the equivalent in Essex to Suffolk Coastal's groups of run-down buildings are its large, individual barns and maltings, often impressive but obsolete structures and a common sight in the northern parts of the county. The council is in a unique position to renovate and convert these economically, and, in appropriate locations, extend its revolving fund into commercial uses, perhaps as starter units for small businesses. By selling the freehold for a management organisation to administer individual leases, the council could recover its capital and still keep to the revolving principle. A joint venture of this type with a development company or a district council might be an attractive extension of the county council's excellent schemes, producing long-term jobs as well as the short-term employment of the building work.

18

Kendal

The Cumbrian town of Kendal has a long and sometimes illustrious history. Catherine Parr, the last wife of Henry VIII, was born in the now ruined Norman castle, the daughter of Thomas Parr, the lord of the castle. The archers in Shakespeare's *Henry IV* wore Kendal Green cloth, the woollen industry having been established in the town in the fourteenth century. Long before that, there was an Anglo-Saxon occupation and before that a Roman camp. Modern Kendal (population 23,000) has diversified its industry into footwear, hosiery, carpets, engineering, insurance, tourism and mint cake. The centre of communications and the market town for a large area, it appears remarkably self-contained with, less remarkably, a strong sense of history; the kind of place which former residents still think of as home and, after enforced absence, return to.

The main street, Highgate, follows the contours of the side of the valley in which the town stands. Off the normally bustling street, tightly packed groups of limestone buildings descend to the River Kent in the valley bottom or climb the hillside in terraced formation, a natural response by the town's builders to the lie of the land. The demolition of many of these distinctive groups of buildings led to the interest by members of the town's civic society in the possible purchase and repair of one of the survivors, Collin Croft.

As its name suggests, the Kendal Civic Society Building Preservation Trust is, like Bradford-on-Avon's, one that developed from the local civic society. Also in common with the Bradford-on-Avon Trust, it took on buildings that appeared destined to soon become a heap of rubble, but whereas in the Wiltshire town there was the benefit of the experience of previous schemes, for the newly fledged Kendal Trust the Collin Croft project was its first. A scheme for Collin Croft had been started by the civic society in 1975, when the society had repaved the length of the stepped right of way, which at one point passes through No 20, on the slope to and from Highgate. Two years later, the listed but crumbling properties became available for purchase. The trust had still to be set up and the £6,700 asking price had to be raised quickly. The civic society responded with a loan of nearly half the sum required and Barclays Bank agreed to lend the remainder. Plans were drawn up for a total of seven dwellings and, on the basis of these, enquiries were made about listed building, town scheme and improvement grants and an Architectural Heritage Fund loan. The enquiries produced positive results: grants alone totalled over £34,000 towards the estimated cost of £110,000.

As well as the very poor condition of the buildings, the newly formed trust had to contend with the steep slope of the site, which produced a scheme with seven different levels and complicated, non-standard internal planning. The positive response of the local authority building regulation officials greatly eased the way towards meeting regulation standards. With the preliminary paperwork completed, the way was clear for construction to start in January 1979. Then followed eighteen months of closely supervised building work; the architect, whose office was only a few minutes' walk away on the other side of Highgate, visited the site at least once a week to deal with the usual blend of bad and good news that is characteristic of renovation work. In the early stages even closer attention was necessary, but fortunately by about the half-way stage, this somewhat nerve-racking process began to take on a more predictable course through to completion in August 1980.

While the work was proceeding, several enquiries were made by would-be purchasers and a local estate agent was appointed to deal with these and final sales. A week before the general release of particulars, the initial enquirers were given the opportunity of first refusal. When the local press announced that the remaining unsold properties were to be for sale to the general public on the following Saturday, over a hundred prospective purchasers turned up and all the properties immediately found buyers.

Two years expired before another opportunity opened up for the trust, again in Collin Croft. This time it was a detached property, substantially Georgian in date and, although not nearly as derelict as the properties had been in the previous scheme, in need of thorough renovation, including substantial rebuilding at the rear. The trust has subdivided the house, forming one property with three bedrooms and one with a single bedroom. Towards the estimated cost of £57,000 the AHF contributed a loan of £20,000, the HBC provided £3,000 in town scheme and restoration grants, there was an improvement grant of £2,000 from the district council and a bank loan of £6,000. Trust capital, boosted by the earlier scheme, made up the rest.

If the Bradford-on-Avon Trust's springboard was in involvement in the social community, the Kendal Trust drew strength from its links with the business community. Its chairman, Peter Crewdson, is head of a family business with the third largest number of employees in the town, and when he took the lead in helping to set up the trust, it was off to a good start. The honorary secretary is a partner in a long-established firm of accountants with offices across the street from those of its architectural adviser, who has lived in the area for forty years and was architect for Collin Croft. Whereas in Bradford-on-Avon there was some difficulty with local bank managers, in Kendal the involvement of the trust's chairman was crucial in obtaining the support of the local branch of Barclays Bank. It was perhaps a combination of knowing who to go to and the council's enlightened attitude that led to the offer of an improvement grant worth £10,600 — not every local authority would have considered buildings in such a poor state as being eligible for an improvement grant. A similar explanation may account for the equally valuable co-operation in respect of building regulations, which could have been a stumbling block but for the positive attitude of the officials, enabling the regulations to be interpreted in favour of the scheme. The trust's business and professional know-how, operating in a town of medium size, was influential. A great strength is that its key figures are involved, irrespective of the trust, in the commercial life of Kendal. Together they saw through a major conservation scheme without even the experience of a less ambitious project.

But if the pattern in other towns is repeated, private developers or individuals, having been shown what is possible, may now take over, though whether they do so with the trust's architectural finesse remains to be seen. This could leave the trust looking for alternative outlets for its skills — perhaps redundant factories or warehousing for either commercial or residential reuse. Perhaps it could widen its search to include a larger area outside Kendal proper, and it might in general terms explore with the local authority ways in which the skills it has to offer can continue to be utilised. Some of this may loosen the trust's ties with the town of Kendal. It could also reduce the benefits of those ties, but any small or medium-sized town trust will, eventually, exhaust the supply of run-down properties that are both suitable and available for renovation within the town itself. To continue, it may need to look outside its parent town, just as the business interests of the officers of the Kendal Trust, although centred on the town, extend beyond its immediate boundaries.

Scotland
LITTLE HOUSES IMPROVEMENT SCHEME

It was concern at apparent official eagerness to destroy older, small houses that led nearly half a century ago to a deputation from the National Trust for Scotland to the Scottish Office and the launching of an appeal for £500,000, a massive sum in those days, to enable small burghal houses to be acquired and restored. The small house, sometimes tiny but often with six or eight rooms, was the product of a Scottish burghal system dating from the twelfth century. To add to royal revenues, burghs, in practice trading communities, were established close to a royal castle; many were on the Lothian and Fife coast where they were able to exploit the fisheries of the River Forth, trade with Scandinavia, the Baltic nations and the Low Countries and have ready access to the markets of two of Scotland's major cities.

For centuries the workplace and home for merchants, burgesses, artisans, shipmasters and fishermen, the little houses were rightly considered by the NTS to be as much a part of Scotland's heritage as its great houses and castles. In 1932, only a year after it was formed, the trust had begun restoring and adapting some of these individually modest, but collectively delightful, houses in the Royal Burgh of Culross, between Glasgow and Edinburgh. The appeal in 1936 was to further this work. Perhaps being over ambitious, it enjoyed only limited success, but the Fourth Marquess of Bute commissioned an Edinburgh architect, Ian Lindsay, to make a survey of buildings in Scotland considered worthy of preservation. The magnitude of the preservation task revealed by this and later surveys, the slowness of the restoration work, the scarcity of funds compared to the heavy capital outlay required and the accelerating decay of the houses all pointed to the need for a fresh initiative.

This came in 1960 when the NTS launched its Little Houses Improvement Scheme and, to make a small budget go further, introduced the United Kingdom to the concept of the revolving fund. The initial capital for the fund was provided by a grant of £10,000 from the Pilgrim Trust[1] and a similar sum from its own general fund. This £20,000, later augmented by £7,500 from Fife County Council, a further £4,000 from the Pilgrim Trust and a £20,000 interest-free loan from a NTS member, was only 4 per cent of the sum that had been considered necessary for the task over twenty years earlier; but it was sufficient to start the renovation of Scotland's little houses, revolving with such speed and effect that since 1960 some 185 buildings, including dwellings, museums and shops, have been restored — work valued at about £2.75 million, well over one hundred times the starting capital. With proceeds from resales, the scheme's accrued capital now stands at over £300,000.

The County of Fife and its burghal towns was at the centre of this activity. The epitome of the Fife little houses is the white harled wall, [2] the red pantile or grey slate roof, forestairs leading to a first-floor doorway[3] and a Dutch gable (the outcome of trading links with the Low

22

Countries), often at right-angles to the street. All these characteristics can be seen in the trust's work in Culross, Kirkcaldy, Dysart, St Monans, Pittenweem and many other Fife towns and villages, but the impetus created by the introduction of the scheme has also permitted a dramatic expansion into other areas throughout Scotland, from Cromarty in the north to the Borders and Ayrshire — the heart of the Burns country.

With a quarter of a century of experience, the Little Houses Improvement Scheme is, in 1985, a well-oiled machine and an important part of the trust's wider activities in looking after Scotland's heritage of buildings and landscape. As this involves staff spread throughout the country, the trust has a ready made intelligence network which, assisted by members, local government officials and others in the planning and property field, enables possible schemes to be quickly identified. In considering the suitability of a property for purchase, the trust's criteria are, in order of priority:

1 Architectural and/or historic merit
2 Purchase price
3 Vacant possession
4 Probable cost of restoration
5 Saleability

It is accepted, therefore, that sometimes buildings are of such great architectural or historic significance that they must be saved, whatever the financial outcome. If this policy results, as it has done, in financial loss in some cases, the trust's firm belief, borne out by practical experience, is that such losses will be balanced by profits elsewhere. In fact, as the build-up of the scheme's capital shows, profits have heavily outweighed losses but, even so, not all buildings at risk can be restored. The final decision on priorities rests with the Management Group (Finance), based at the trust's Edinburgh headquarters. To help it reach its decisions, advice and data are provided by surveyors, architects, lawyers and accountants, each responsible for different aspects of the work.

Once buildings have been designated for conservation and purchased, the trust mainly adopts one of three methods:

Trust Restorations Where buildings are of outstanding importance, as part of an attractive group or in their own right, are in danger of rapid and serious deterioration and, if restored, a market exists which would enable them to be resold, the trust will itself restore, using its revolving fund. The Black Bull in Old Dumbarton Road at Kippen, Stirlingshire, completed in January 1984, was renovated by this method. It was the first of the little houses projects to seek and obtain assistance from the AHF.

Restoring Owner Buildings may be purchased from the trust's property bank and restored by the new owner. Members are able to inform the trust of their requirements and receive notification at regular intervals of suitable properties available for purchase, either owned by or known to the trust. Conditions of sale require:

1 That restoration will start within a given time.
2 That plans must be approved by the trust before restoration begins.
3 That the owner must sign a Conservation Agreement to ensure the continued protection of the building once work has been completed.

No 4 West Shore, St Monans, is an example of restoration by an owner.

Restoring Purchaser This is similar to the previous method except that the restoration of the building is handled by the trust's professional staff, the trust becoming a restoring agent with the costs, fees and building work met by the purchaser. Before work commences the purchaser/client signs an agreement so as to ensure payment for abortive work should, for some reason, the purchaser/client decide not to proceed after the preparation of plans and costings. The work at 15 East Shore, St Monans was carried out by the trust on behalf of a purchaser.

In addition to these three principal methods, there are also joint local authority/trust revolving funds, where the trust acts as restoring agent; local preservation society renovation schemes are assisted by interest-free loans from the trust, and recently joint schemes have been set up with housing authorities. Under this last arrangement, the housing authority conveys derelict but architecturally attractive buildings to the trust at no cost on the understanding that the net profit, if any, resulting from resale will be shared equally. The terrace at 1–4 Hepworth Lane in Forres, Morayshire has been restored by this method. Whichever method is adopted, the eventual purchaser of the renovated property is always required to enter into a Conservation Agreement.

Since 1938, the trust has been empowered to enter into Conservation Agreements with purchasers which, whilst not precluding sale or gift, constitute a true burden on property in perpetuity. Every completed restoration is covered by such an agreement, which includes the following conditions:

1 The plans must be approved by the trust and the restoration professionally supervised
2 Certain enumerated internal and external features must be retained
3 The façade must not be altered without permission and proper maintenance must be carried out internally and externally
4 Immediate sale for profit is not to be undertaken
5 The trust plaque will be displayed

Plates 1 and 2 Before renovation 5–8 Market Street, Bradford-on-Avon was an empty shell and an eyesore but within a year it had been transformed into a showpiece. For most people in the town, its previously hidden charm was revealed for the first time *(Bradford-on-Avon Preservation Trust/Photography West)*

Plate 5 The footpath that climbs the hillside from the main shopping street in Kendal passes underneath No. 20 Collin Croft, one of the group of stone buildings given a new lease of life by the Kendal Civic Society Building Preservation Trust *(Kendal Civic Society Building Preservation Trust/Anthony Price)*

Plates 3 and 4 With disastrous visual results the Old Coffee House in Manningtree, Essex, had been altered and patched up many times before Essex County Council decided to purchase the property for its revolving-fund programme *(Essex County Council/Stanland)*

Additions or amendments under 2 and 3 may, in certain circumstances, be undertaken but only with the specific agreement of the trust. Under 4 the trust retains a right of pre-emption for five years and a right of inspection every five years and on change of ownership. The plaque mentioned in 5 is provided in various forms applicable to Restoring Owners, Restoring Purchasers or purchasers of trust restorations.

Perhaps the most ambitious scheme to date is being developed on the shores of Loch Lomond. Built as a model village between 1850 and 1860 to very precise design standards, the village of Luss, Strathclyde, set between the loch and the hills, is a place of great beauty. It is an outstanding conservation area and popular with tourists. The Luss Estates Company found that it was unable to maintain the stone and slate cottages to an acceptable standard, and in 1979 the company approached the trust with a view to offering it thirty of the cottages. Since the sums involved were too great for the trust to fund alone, it successfully put forward the idea of a consortium to tackle the project, consisting of Dumbarton District Council, Strathclyde Regional Council[4] and the World of Property Housing Trust Scottish Housing Association Ltd. Initially, two cottages were purchased by the NTS using their Strathclyde region joint revolving fund. A price for a further twenty-five cottages was negotiated by the District Valuer and all are being restored by the WPHT over a three-year period, with funds provided through the Housing Corporation, members of the consortium, including the trust, and the Historic Buildings Council for Scotland. Although it is unlikely that there would be any difficulty in selling the cottages, the consortium realised that, because of their attraction as holiday homes, selling them would put at risk the social homogeneity of the village so the cottages are being leased to existing occupiers.

In the Little Houses Improvement Scheme, the NTS has a lively offspring. The scheme has given the trust a dynamic and imaginative face, while the influence and respected image of the trust opens doors and lends status to the scheme's work. It is clearly an effective combination. The concepts of the revolving fund and restoring purchasers and owners have spread throughout the United Kingdom, but the Scottish achievement, rooted in its National Trust, will be a difficult one to improve upon in the field of domestic, vernacular buildings. After twenty-five years, the Little Houses Improvement Scheme is part of the

Plates 6 and 7 Few people would have included The Gyles, Pittenween, among Scotland's rich heritage before the National Trust for Scotland took it under its wing as part of its Little Houses Improvement Scheme *(National Trust for Scotland)*

system, operating at all levels with an eye to aesthetics, as well as business, civic society and estate agency rolled into one. The trust's membership, now over 110,000, provides a firm bedrock of support. It gives advice and financial help to local societies and trusts, produces attractive and informative publications and has an established pattern of key meetings with influential people to help maintain momentum. There seems no reason why this should not be sustained over another twenty-five years and perhaps extended to include other characteristic building types in need of care and also of importance to Scotland's rich heritage, great houses and even castles included.

Suffolk

Victor Gordon was a member of Suffolk Coastal District Council for only a few months, but in that short time he put forward an idea that was to develop in the years 1975–82, on the 'purchase, renovate and sell' revolving basis, into a £700,000 building conservation programme. The council was newly established as part of the 1974 reorganisation of local government and Councillor Gordon's suggestion of a positive council role in the acquisition and repair of run-down old buildings came at a time when it was particularly receptive to ideas that would fit in with its motto, 'New views to life'. The idea coincided with a similar proposal made by the council's newly appointed planning officer, John Hansen, and so £25,000 was allocated from the capital reserves for a revolving fund to be administered by the council's planning committee, for just such a newish view.

A policy for the use of the fund evolved on a step-by-step basis. The intention was to use it to renovate old properties with architectural appeal that otherwise would remain in disrepair. To maximise public benefit, it seemed sensible to concentrate on the town areas rather than the countryside, an approach that also coincided with the wish to optimise the chances, best in town conservation areas, of historic buildings grant aid. The need to recoup the capital and the desire to limit ongoing after-sales involvement in properties suggested the sale of completed schemes freehold. For this reason, and because the housing sector made up much the largest and most predictable part of the market, it was decided to concentrate on residential use. It was also decided that, although it could carry out much of the initial appraisal work itself, the council did not possess the specialist resources needed for this type of work among its own staff, and so consultant architects and quantity surveyors of proven ability in the conservation field would be invited to help as necessary.

30

The choice of schemes would inevitably be influenced, though not determined, by selling prices which varied considerably throughout the district, and in order to get the fund off to the best possible start it was thought desirable that the first scheme should be in a town with relatively high market appeal.

NEW STREET, WOODBRIDGE

An opportunity to put theory into practice arose in the woebegone shape of a row of cottages in New Street, Woodbridge. The cottages probably made up a more substantial scheme than had been envisaged when the fund was set up but, using the revolving technique, it would be possible to carry it out in phases, and so finish up with a single project worth several times the available seed-corn money. It soon became obvious that substantial areas of streets could be improved in this way and that the result could have considerable market appeal and impact, much greater than the renovation of an individual property.

Nothing could have been more appropriate than that the district council should take on the renovation of the New Street cottages, since their derelict state was the outcome of actions by predecessor local authorities. Most were already in local-authority ownership, six having been acquired for a long-abandoned road widening scheme and passed to Suffolk County Council at the 1974 reorganisation. Others, purchased under the Public Health Acts, were owned by the district council. Acquisitions had started in pre-war years and the street had been in decline ever since, at first directly threatened by the road widening line which involved the cottages' demolition and more recently, when the widening was abandoned, by the less obvious but equally blighting proposal in the county council's 1971 Town Map to replace the attractive Edwardian school buildings on adjoining land by a decked car park and access road to serve the central shopping area. Although it seemed unlikely that the Town Map proposals would ever be implemented, in 1975 the Town Map remained the official planning document and there was no chance of its early revision. It was, therefore, necessary to devise a detailed plan in conjunction with the county council, that would meet the requirements of the Town Map but safeguard the immediate outlook from the cottages in the improbable event of the decked car park being constructed. The outcome was the agreement of the county council to a plan which routed the car park traffic well away from the cottages and interposed an area of open space.

This was one of several matters in which county and district councils worked closely together. Both councils had an interest in seeing the

31

cottages renovated. The school was the responsibility of the county council and, for as long as anyone could remember, the cottages had formed a dilapidated 70yds of its northern boundary, presenting a dismal outlook from the classroom windows and the playground. For this reason, the school's headmaster was particularly keen to see the district council's plans proceed. When it came to negotiating the transfer of a small part of the school land for inclusion in the renovation scheme there were no difficulties, and even arrangements for the storage of building materials on part of the school playground and vehicle access across it were agreed. Towards the end of the scheme, as its contribution, the county highways department offered to repave the footpath in front of the cottages in brick paviors so as to be more in keeping with their character than the normal tarmac or concrete.

Negotiations between the two councils' respective valuers for the transfer to the district of the county's six properties proceeded against a background of similar goodwill and were quickly concluded. Because of their very poor condition, the basis for valuation was site value, both for these and for the cottages that had to be appropriated from the council's housing account. It was estimated that the renovation cost would be equivalent to the cost of new houses of similar area so there was no value in the buildings themselves.

In the first survey of historic buildings in Woodbridge, the cottages had been listed Grade III, but with the phasing out of this category, they were not thought to be of sufficient interest to upgrade to II and so were omitted from the new list entirely. Even so, the cottages formed a picturesque group, particularly at the rear, with their many roof pitches and materials, the earliest probably dating from the seventeenth century and the majority late eighteenth or early nineteenth century. For these reasons, and for their contribution to the street scene, informal discussions about grant aid produced a favourable response from the historic buildings section of the DoE.

Thus encouraged, the council adopted a report from its officers in May 1975 recommending that a draft, costed scheme should be prepared by consultant architects, with a view to the later preparation of detailed proposals, working drawings and bills of quantities for the initial phase. Approval to the detailed stage of four properties followed in November.

In February 1976, a building contractors' tender list was drawn up following an advertisement in the local paper, inviting interested contractors to notify the council. Twenty contractors replied and from these the consultant selected eight for interview to explain to them the intentions of the scheme and to assess their reaction and capacity to carry it out. The eight selected were asked to complete a questionnaire, to visit the site before interview and were sent a preliminary drawing of the proposals. Each interview lasted about half an hour and shorthand notes were taken to record what was said.[1] Representatives of the council, the consultant architects and quantity surveyors attended.

As well as revealing the contractors' general attitude to the project, the interviews also gave an indication of how much control there would be on important items such as joinery manufacture, the readiness to acquire and work with second-hand materials, which parts of the work would be let to subcontractors and how the job would be administered. This would lead, hopefully, to the appointment of one who would be reliable and have appropriately skilled craftsmen to call on. A transcript of the interviews with two of the contractors is included under 'Selecting a Builder' in Part 2.

Out of the eight contractors interviewed, six were invited to tender. One month was allowed for the preparation of tenders, which were opened on 27 May 1976. Formal approval by the council of the lowest tender followed in July, and 16 August 1976 was the date set for the start of the work on site by the successful contractor on the basis of a forty-week contract. Press notices resulted in the first enquiries about the project from other councils.

By the time building work had started on the first four cottages in Phase 1, the consultant architects had a scheme well in hand for the remainder. The council's ownership was broken by three privately owned properties at two sections of the New Street frontage. One of these was owner-occupied by an elderly lady and was in relatively good order. The architects advised that the inclusion of this property was not essential to the scheme, so the possibility of acquisition by the council was not pursued — the owner subsequently carried out her own improvement scheme using the same firms of architects and contractors as the council and also obtained grant aid from the HBC. The other properties were a pair, one including a fish and chip shop, and were for sale. In this case it was considered that the overall scheme would benefit from their inclusion, the shop being converted back into the house it had originally been. With these two extra properties, it was decided that the scheme should comprise three phases instead of two.

Providing that work in Phase 1 proceeded smoothly, early starts on the remaining phases would positively demonstrate confidence in the scheme and encourage prospective purchasers. At about the half-way stage in the first phase, with the contractor performing well, the council decided to set aside its standing orders to allow tenders to be negotiated with the contractor already established on site, so that by the time Phase 1 was finished the next phase would be under way. It was thought particularly important to get the sales of the first properties off to a good start and, from the point of view of sales, the timing of the completion of Phase 1 in late spring/early summer, normally the best period for house sales, worked well.

By February 1977 more than thirty enquiries had been received from would-be purchasers, and the council discussed methods of sale against a background of optimism. It was decided to offer the first completed cottage for sale by tender, providing that the best price offered both exceeded the district valuer's valuation and the cost of the work. To the public, expecting to be told the asking price, as in any normal house purchase, this method turned out to be unpopular and in the event no acceptable offers were received. When the prices were fixed at £15,750–£17,750 (1977 prices), sales followed quickly.

As part of the publicity for the scheme, a formal opening was planned for a Wednesday in May — early-closing day in Woodbridge when there would be less traffic than usual in the busy street. A buffet lunch was provided by the general contractor. District councillors and chief officers, representatives of every local authority in Suffolk, the media and the headmaster of the primary school were among those invited. This was an opportunity for members of the council to see the work at first hand at different stages — complete (Phase 1), early on (Phase 2) and not yet started (Phase 3). A local nursery landscaped the small gardens and one of its employees, evidently enthused by the scheme, gave a gleditschia tree for the front garden of the end cottage. The chairman of the planning committee was interviewed by local television and appeared in that evening's news programme. The council's planning officer was interviewed for local radio news.

Following the opening, one of the cottages was equipped as a sales office for two months. For this comparatively short period a fully furnished showhouse was considered too ambitious, although an estimate was obtained from an Ipswich store, but a table and chairs, some kitchen equipment lent by local showrooms, a small display of drawings of the scheme and some potted plants helped to give the cottage a more lived-in appearance. The drawings included suggestions of how the cottage could look when furnished. The cottage was manned on a rota basis by planning department staff, who produced a low-cost descriptive brochure.

Although at this stage only four properties were completed, the

34

publicity from the opening day and the subsequent public viewing period from May to July effectively sold all eleven cottages in the scheme even before prices had been fixed for the majority of them. In all, 240 enquiries were received from prospective purchasers. The first promotion of the scheme took place at an ideal time of year; even though Phase 2 completion of another four cottages came in the depths of winter in January 1978, the sales momentum from the previous summer had its effect — the first purchaser took possession on 22 February — and it was now looking as though sales revenue would more than cover the council's costs. The final group of properties was completed in August and three months later all were sold and occupied.

There are four footnotes: the first concerns the residential density of the scheme. Following the public examination of the Suffolk County Council's submitted County Structure Plan Written Statement, the Secretary of State modified the paragraph concerning housing density as follows:

> The Panel suggested that densities of 8–12 dwellings per acre (as proposed in the Written Statement) might be rather low . . . When the Secretary of State proposed a modification aimed at securing a higher overall density, the County Council and several district councils objected on the grounds that a gross density of 10–15 dwellings . . . was really only suited to estate or urban development and should apply only to such development. The Secretary of State has considered these points sympathetically, but, noting that the Written Statement as submitted itself provides considerable scope for discretion in the administration of the density policy, and that the settlement policy provides for development to be concentrated in the towns, has concluded that it is reasonable to seek *overall* a gross density of 10–15 dwellings per acre . . .

Including the privately owned property in the middle, the twelve dwellings and seven car parking spaces in the New Street renovation scheme, seven properties with two bedrooms and five with three bedrooms, provide a gross density on 0.39 of an acre of 30.3 dwellings per acre. Even taking the Secretary of State's higher range of densities, the New Street scheme appears to have produced twice the number of properties that would normally be built on the same area of land in a redevelopment. Purchasers, significantly, were not deterred.

Secondly, two privately sponsored renovation/rebuild projects in Woodbridge soon followed. One, a terrace of half a dozen red-brick cottages, followed very much the New Street pattern in that they had been empty and run-down for many years, and in the manner of conversion there was a hint of the New Street style. The other was part-renovation and part-new work. The architects for the scheme were the same as for the council's. The developer must have considered this a selling point as it was mentioned in an advertising feature in the local paper. The timing and the manner in which they were carried out suggest that neither scheme would have taken place without the example of New Street. It was also noticeable that the privately owned properties on the north side of New Street, facing the council scheme, began to look more cared for, perhaps a reflection of their sharp increase in market value directly attributable to the New Street project.

Thirdly, having been omitted in the 1971 Woodbridge list of buildings of architectural or historic interest, the cottages were reinstated in an amendment to the list as Grade II. And finally, admittedly at a time of high inflation, the prices realised, £15,750–£20,000, compared with a local estate agent's estimate at feasibility stage of £8,500–£12,500.

ANGEL YARD, SAXMUNDHAM

At the half-way stage in New Street, with the scheme making encouraging progress, thoughts began to turn to a successor. A redundant public house in Saxmundham provided the answer; known as the Angel Inn, it was a former coaching inn of sixteenth-century origin, timber framed and Grade II listed. It had been on the open market for some time. To motorists passing through the market town on the A12 trunk road, the Angel Inn was one of a small group of buildings that formed a bottleneck and slowed traffic. To most of the inhabitants, it was a run-down eyesore. To the planner it was a key part of the town's conservation area with two important frontages, one to the busy High Street and the other to the quieter Market Place, only crowded with stalls and people on Wednesday market days. More of a working town than a show-piece, Saxmundham house prices were lower than in Wood-bridge: Saxmundham's were approximately 15 per cent lower, but it was realised that the revolving fund, to be effective, had to operate in a range of market conditions. A scheme for the Angel, surrounded by properties in a variety of conditions, could have the effect of revitalising a large part of the town centre.

The Angel is in the centre of a narrow island block. When, in August 1977, the council began to take an interest, all the properties in the

Plates 8 and 9 The demolition of the end cottage *(top)* in New Street, Woodbridge, surprisingly revealed large gable window arches *(below)*, showing that the demolished cottage had been a later addition *(Feilden & Mawson and Suffolk Coastal District Council)*

block on the north side of the Angel were either for sale or were the subject of proposed improvements by the shopkeeper owner. It was quickly apparent that, if the council were to buy the properties for sale and the owner of the rest was willing, it would be possible to rearrange the ownership boundaries with advantages to both parties. By an exchange of land and buildings, the shopkeeper could have a better commercial position and the council the opportunity to include in its residential scheme the properties adjoining the Angel. Although this would increase the cost of the scheme, the council had already adopted the technique of completion in stages in New Street and there seemed no reason why a similar approach should not be used in Saxmundham.

Agreement was reached with the adjoining owner on this basis and, after the council had satisfied itself about the feasibility of the scheme in general terms, its consultant architects were asked to prepare detailed proposals. The New Street project was still about nine months from completion, but the council wished to see continuity of work, and even a small overlap between the two contracts was considered to be acceptable.

In the period up to spring 1978, details of the land exchange were finalised and tender documents were prepared for the first phase of four dwellings. One of the units gave rise to complications. It adjoined a furnishers and the owner wished to incorporate it, refurbished by the council, into his shop premises. Negotiations proceeded for several months but eventually came to nothing. Conversion of this unit into a single dwelling, because of its elongated shape, produced an unsatisfactory and expensive plan. An alternative was devised, producing a small shop on the Market Place frontage and a dwelling behind but, although an attractive plan, this too was a relatively expensive arrangement. Meanwhile tenders were received on the basis of four dwellings. They were well above the figures that had been forecast only a few months earlier, but by renovating the whole of the fourth unit as a shop and avoiding the need to provide the services and fittings that would be necessary in a dwelling, it would be possible to bring the lowest tender figure more in line with the forecast. The market demand for a shop unit could not be guaranteed but the commercial location was good, and if the property proved unsaleable as a shop it would be possible to revert

Plates 10 and 11 When it was purchased by Suffolk Coastal District Council, parts of the Regency Works House, Leiston, *(above)* were near to collapse *(Suffolk Coastal District Council)*. The patchwork quilt roof of the redundant and dilapidated Angel Inn, Saxmundham, was and is a distinctive feature *(below)* to the original idea for a dwelling, notwithstanding its disadvantages. It was decided to proceed on the basis of Phase 1 comprising three dwellings and one shop. Bearing in mind current house prices and the likely increases up to the time the properties would be available for purchase, it was considered that such a scheme, taking into account conservation area grant aid offered by the Civic Trust[2], might break even.

By the spring of 1978 the New Street project was close to completion. To mark the event and to give publicity to the successor project, the council decided to put together a travelling exhibition, opening in Woodbridge's best-known landmark, the Tide Mill, in July and then touring the district throughout the summer. Arrangements were made for it to be shown for two-week periods at Aldeburgh Moot Hall, Framlingham Castle and Snape Maltings, as well as Woodbridge, Barclays Bank in Saxmundham and the Spa Pavilion and public library at Felixstowe. Opening on 17 July, the exhibition was planned to run until 14 October. A preview was held at the Tide Mill for the press, council members and officers, representatives of other local authorities and New Street purchasers. Although towards the end of the tour, the novelty of setting up and striking the exhibition in its different locations was beginning to fade, it presented a positive aspect of the council's work and was well received. The planning officer reported to his committee in October that the exhibition in its three-month tour had been seen by about 10,000 people, one of whom shortly afterwards asked for the largest of the Saxmundham dwellings to be reserved — the building work was in the very early stages and the council was unable to quote a price until it was completed and values could be assessed almost a year later. With magazine articles that summer and autumn in the *Illustrated London News, Country Life, House and Garden* and technical journals, the Suffolk conservation schemes began to be noted further afield.

The first of the monthly site meetings between client, architect and builder took place at the Angel in September 1978. With a reliable working foreman, the monthly meeting at New Street, supplemented by inspections in between by the architect and council staff, had been found to give adequate monitoring and supervision of the work. The same formula was adopted at the Angel. Even the client, architect, builder team was the same, the lowest tender having been submitted by the New Street builder. In fact, the builder's team transferred intact, along with the same positive working relationship between all parties that had developed in New Street.

At the end of 1978, the council's revolving fund was operating at several levels. The sales of the last three cottages in New Street were nearing completion, negotiations for the transfer to the council of additional properties adjoining the Angel Inn were being finalised, and a tender was being negotiated with the building contractor for the second phase. Progress on the first phase was being held up by bad weather and particularly cramped working conditions, but the extension of the site to include the extra properties gave the contractor more working room, showing the advantage of merging the two contracts so that the building trades could work through the properties in an orderly sequence. Although the original intention had been to carry out the work in two separate phases, the council, encouraged by the offer of further grant assistance via the Civic Trust and the early signs of interest by purchasers in Phase 1, saw the sense of running both together, and at the end of November 1978 a tender for the remaining part of the scheme was accepted. If the contracts kept reasonably to schedule, the Saxmundham project would be completed by the following autumn, and if completion was to be marked by an exhibition on the New Street pattern, containing details of the next scheme, it was time, about twelve months in advance, to consider suitable properties for a third project. The exhibition, in October 1979, included outline proposals for a scheme 4 miles from Saxmundham, which was to be a new departure for the revolving fund — the conversion of a group of redundant industrial buildings in Leiston, Suffolk's only Victorian company town.

With the scope of the Angel scheme extended, it was renamed Angel Yard. It naturally produced a wider range of accommodation than New Street, the Angel itself subdividing into the shop, two dwellings with three bedrooms and one with two bedrooms, while the adjoining cottages were reshaped into three smaller properties, one having two bedrooms and the two others with one bedroom. Some of the smaller dwellings had attic spaces forming gallery areas with ladder access above the bedrooms. It was envisaged that the range of dwelling types would produce a range of property values and so extend their appeal in an uncertain market. To widen the range of values even further, the heating specification varied from full gas-fired central heating in the larger dwellings, each with at least one open fireplace, to basic gas fires and water heaters in the three smallest cottages. This was intended to bring the smaller units within the range of the first-time buyer.

The contract had its alarming moments and share of difficulties. There were substantial areas of defective timber, and while these were repaired, parts of the building had to be supported on temporary props. Much of the work alongside the trunk road, including a new crinkle-crankle wall[3] to screen the gardens, was carried out in difficult con-

41

ditions because of the heavy traffic; at off-peak periods the trunk road had to be closed and the traffic diverted, involving liaison with the high-way authority and the police. Industrial action affected the delivery of copper tubing and gas meters, and for about three and a half months progress was impeded by exceptionally inclement weather. The original completion date of July 1979 was at first put back to September, but Phase 1 was only finally completed in October and Phase 2 in January 1980.

The October 1979 exhibition was held in the shop unit and a formal opening, performed by the Duke and Duchess of Grafton, was arranged for 9 October. This was a repeat of the similar occasion in Woodbridge. Because it was late in the year, the exhibition was reduced to two weeks.

These [Angel Yard, Saxmundham] are officially due to come on the market round about the publication date of this issue of The Countryman — but if you are tempted, do not be too optimistic. Already, by May, the local grapevine had worked so effectively that four of the six were reserved . . .

Tony Aldous, *The Countryman*, autumn 1979

Owing to the withdrawal of the purchaser at a late stage on two occasions, the sale of one of the dwellings was considerably delayed, completion of the sale taking place more than twelve months after the completion of the building work. By July 1980 the shop had found a buyer. Otherwise, completion of sale and occupation followed approximately six months after the properties had been renovated, except for the purchaser who had made a reservation late in 1978 at the time of the previous exhibition. She moved in first, hard on the heels of the builder in October 1979. One of the small cottages was sold to a first-time purchaser. Another was sold for commercial use as an opticians.

The completed scheme finally comprised two properties in business use and five dwellings. Including half the width of adjoining roads, the five dwellings without on-site car parking spaces, occupy 0.15 of an acre, a density of 33.33 dwellings per acre. Adding a notional area of 0.0325 of an acre for a block of five garages with parking space in front, the density was 27.40 dwellings per acre.

The need for parking spaces and garages was debated throughout the progress of the scheme. To have incorporated them within the site would have torn the buildings apart. At first, it was considered that spaces should be set aside and a covered area provided in the adjoining council-owned public car park, which was only extensively used on market days, but objection to this proposal led to consideration of the purchase of a separate piece of land in the vicinity to construct a block of lock-up garages. By this time, purchasers were expressing interest but the demand for parking or garage space appeared slight, so the idea of purchasing the extra piece of land was dropped. Any purchaser wishing to was able to acquire a licence to park in the public car park. Probably more by accident than design, the car-parking provision reflected purchasers' needs which turned out, in this town centre position, to be less than had been anticipated.

HIGH GREEN, LEISTON

There were no uncertainties of this sort in the next scheme, at Leiston, where the site was larger and the inclusion of a garage area the least of its problems. Thoughts about a revolving-fund scheme at Leiston went back to 1977, when Cecil Lightfoot, a member of the Suffolk Preservation Society and a former Clerk of East Suffolk County Council, put forward proposals for the preservation of one of the town's redundant and largest buildings, the somewhat curiously named Long Shop. Lofty and galleried rather than long, it was built in 1852 for the exclusive production of portable steam engines, as part of the massive Richard Garrett Town Works. The society's idea was to use the Long Shop and other redundant buildings for an engineering museum telling the story — unlikely in the heart of rural Suffolk — of the Richard Garrett enterprise, at that time still in business on another site in the town. Having estimated the museum's requirements, it was evident that more buildings existed than it could realistically use; all were originally part of the Town Works complex and occupied over 2 acres, fronting Main Street, of the original 7 acre site in the centre of the town. One of the surplus properties, the Grade II listed Works House, had been built in 1826 by one of the several Richard Garretts for himself and his family. With its three floors and formal Regency elevation, it therefore had special significance in the context of the museum, as well as prominence in the Leiston street scene. The Works House was one of an interconnecting group of buildings, formerly used as workshops, offices and storage, occupying about 1 acre of land to the east of the proposed museum. To the west had stood the former Works Institute, built by the company in 1861 as a social centre for the town. The only remaining feature in 1977 was the imposing façade to Main Street.

The district council was one of the parties to the talks about the museum. At the time these were first taking place, the council was about halfway through the Woodbridge scheme and only just beginning to sense the possible scope for later use of its infant revolving fund. What it could do, and did, was to improve the local climate for renova-

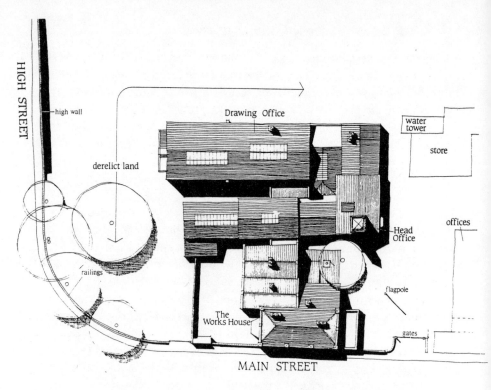

HIGH STREET

high wall

derelict land

Drawing Office

water tower

store

railings

Head Office

offices

flagpole

The Works House

gates

MAIN STREET

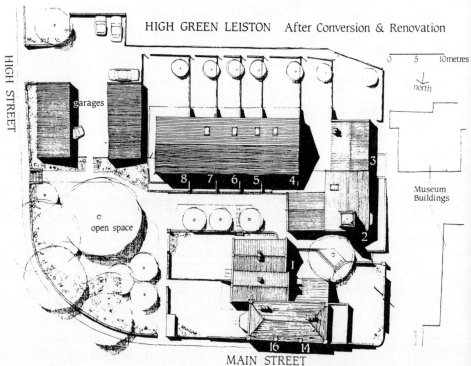

HIGH GREEN LEISTON   After Conversion & Renovation

HIGH STREET

garages

0   5   10metres

north

open space

8   7   6   5   4

3

Museum Buildings

2

1

16   14

MAIN STREET

Fig 1 Plans for the rehabilitation of part of the Richard Garrett Works at Leiston in Suffolk

tion by the designation of a conservation area covering the redundant Garrett properties and other of the older streets of Leiston. Meanwhile, the Works House and its related buildings were noted as possible revolving-fund material. When the time came, late in 1978, to examine the possibilities in more detail, the museum was still in its formative stages and the whole site, for sale but arousing little interest, had a distinctly unwanted look.

By now, the feasibility exercise was taking on a familiar pattern. With the museum also on the look-out for financial support, the two projects could be considered as one for the purposes of grant eligibility. This was advantageous, even though the museum project was bound to proceed at a slower pace than the council's, for it gave an extra dimension to both. Conservation area status covering the unlisted buildings also helped grant prospects. The site could be planned as a whole and visual requirements could be of at least equal importance as ownership boundaries. The gain to the town, unfashionably Victorian and not figuring prominently on Suffolk's tourist map, would be considerable.

Events beyond the council's control were to make the gain even greater than had been foreseen. In 1980, two years after celebrating its bicentenary and within a few days of completing the sale to the council of the properties for the revolving-fund exercise, the affairs of the ailing Richard Garrett Engineering Co were placed in the hands of the receiver and the jobs of most of its 500 workers, amounting to probably 20 per cent of the working population of the town, were lost. Other firms moved in, and out again. Leiston, Suffolk's boom town of the middle years of the nineteenth century, became the depressed town of the 1980s. Ironically enough, its problems were aggravated by the proposal of the town's only remaining major industrial employer, the Central Electricity Generating Board, to build a second nuclear power station nearby at Sizewell, on the one hand holding the promise of many new jobs but on the other effectively placing key investment decisions, that might have reinvigorated the town, in abeyance until it had been decided whether or not the power station development was to proceed.

Because of this, the feasibility stage balance sheet looked better than the final figures, the reverse of the Woodbridge and Saxmundham experience, but even at feasibility stage the project looked risky. It was known that the market in Leiston was weak in comparison with most in the district and, in contrast to Woodbridge, house prices were dramatically low. Since the cost of building work was unlikely to be very different from anywhere else in the district, the return on sales seemed likely to be poor when set against the renovation costs. Against this, the council had done well out of its previous schemes and the revolving fund was worth several times its starting capital. There seemed to be little prospect of any other organisation carrying out a scheme of the kind required and there was no doubt that a worthwhile improvement would result, affecting not just the Garrett buildings but others in the vicinity as well.

The building contract was planned over two years in two phases, with finishing dates in spring or early summer to allow for the viewing of completed houses in good weather and to improve the chances of sales. Although theoretically the council was not obliged to proceed with Phase 2 if the first went badly, it realised that the scheme was in reality a cohesive single project and that the decision to proceed with the first phase, the Works House, was, in effect, a commitment to complete both. Work started a little behind schedule in July 1980, owing to delays in completing the purchase of the properties, and the first of the fortnightly client/architect/builder site meetings, normally also attended by the quantity surveyor, was held. Throughout most of the contract period, weekly site visits by the architect were also necessary to achieve the required degree of supervision.

The Works House had a few surprises in store. The external elevations were all in Suffolk gault bricks, but up to first-floor level it was found that the main structure was flint, panelled to give a plaster finish internally. An ancient oak frame, dating from perhaps the sixteenth century, was discovered in an internal wall, a rare find in Victorian Leiston. Parts of the rear of the house were found to be unsafe and were completely rebuilt, but the Soane-like cast-iron acroteria,[4] which it was feared might need to be recast, came up like new when sandblasted. Already two houses as built by Richard Garrett with a pair of doors to Main Street, the Works House now became three houses, two each with four to five bedrooms and one with two. The bigger houses were large for a modest working town but there was little alternative — houses with high, spacious rooms and large, shuttered sash windows have a period character that can only be acknowledged and respected, whatever the vagaries of market demand.

Local residents followed the progress of building work with interest. With the contractor's agreement, the local high school adopted the renovation work as a subject for its art classes and the results formed part of the exhibition that was held in the completed Works House in July 1981. The school also provided the singers and players for a musical evening, attended by town and district councillors, at the Works House early in July, but the main event of the month, on 17 July, was the formal opening by HRH the Duke of Gloucester. With the town still barely recovered from the shock of Garrett's closure, the opening of the Works House took on the nature of a defiant celebration, something to cheer about in bad times.

It was planned so as to involve the town as a whole: the town's shops lent hardware for the kitchen and indoor plants, the town council contributed a working model of a Garrett steam engine and a marble bust of Richard Garrett, along with a collection of his top hats. Tables and chairs and a table lamp were borrowed from further afield, and seagrass matting took the bare look from the floorboards. Much the largest item came from an environmentally aware piano dealer in Ipswich who, free of charge, transported a grand piano the 25 miles to and from Leiston. In this way, and at no cost to the council, the Works House was prepared for the exhibition and opening. The exhibition took different forms and themes in the different rooms of one of the larger houses. On the ground floor, the proposals for the remainder of the scheme were shown, along with drawings and photographs of the schemes at Woodbridge and Saxmundham. One room on the first floor featured the museum project and in another drawings by local schoolchildren of work in progress. The cellar was equipped as a miniature film theatre, with seating borrowed from Leiston Middle School, for a slide show and recorded commentary about renovation work countrywide.

The afternoon of Friday, 17 July 1981, was a time to remember for every child of school age in Leiston for, instead of classroom lessons, there was route-lining duty, the opportunity to cheer louder than your neighbour or, alternatively, listen to the brass of the Leiston British Legion Band, playing in Old Post Office Square in front of the Works House, all in honour of HRH the Duke of Gloucester. Although members of the royal family were thought to have passed through the town on a number of occasions, it was the first time, it seemed, that one had made a special visit. For a brief moment, Leiston was in flag-waving and bunting mood. In addition to the hundreds of Leiston faces, the royal visitor was able to see work in three areas — the completed Works House, the second phase a few months into the contract, and the museum, still in its embryonic stage.

The July exhibition and opening produced publicity both locally and nationally and much favourable comment for the scheme but also the first signs of sales resistance so far in the council's revolving-fund programme, even though the Works House was undoubtedly the most distinguished building in the series. However, in 1981 it stood on a building site and it was possible that, as the whole site became tidier, the purchasers would appear. There was no question of stopping or delaying work. The second phase had started in February 1981, and for the most part was proving to be more straightforward than had been the first; six of its seven houses were of two or three bedrooms and considered likely to be in greater demand in Leiston than the larger properties in the Works House. But by the end of the year it seemed that the momentum of interest engendered by the summer activities was fading, with none of the three properties in the Works House sold, and agents were appointed with a view to marketing the whole project of ten houses in spring 1982.

Site works in Phase 2 revealed some of the less helpful aspects of Garrett's industrial legacy in the shape of underground brick and concrete structures. To assist in their removal, a grant under the derelict land scheme was obtained from the DoE.[5] The site works were an important element of the scheme, which included the landscaping as a public open space of the rounded corner where Leiston's High Street and Main Street meet. Raised a few feet above the general street level and already having the benefit of a group of mature trees, the open space, with buildings on all four sides, was a useful bonus for a town lacking similar spaces in its centre. The name High Green was thereby suggested and adopted.

The building work in Phase 2 comprised the subdivision of the turn-of-the-century drawing office/workshop to form a terrace of five houses and the construction of two houses from the company head office. Within a sound brick-and-a-half shell, the former was easily and economically achieved. The head office was a different matter: originally, it appeared to have been a single-storey building because the ground-floor walls, partly flint faced, were mainly load-bearing, but the first floor had a cast-iron-reinforced timber frame, surmounted by a clock tower. The first-floor construction was of a similar type to the Long Shop of 1852, but the ground-floor alterations revealed a brick inscribed 'S.G. 1823', probably the initials of Richard Garrett's wife, Sarah. Part of the head office, therefore, predated by three years the building of the Works House. As the work proceeded the interest of its structure in relation to the development of the Town Works became increasingly apparent. So did its poor condition and the cost of making it sound.

By the time Phase 2 was complete in July 1982, a local initiative had secured the future of the Works Institute façade as the Main Street elevation of a new building for the town's medical group practice and clinic, the Long Shop had been completely reroofed and an independent trust had been established to run the museum. The spring sales effort had produced moderate interest, but only two uncompleted sales. The council and its agents decided to set up a sales office in one of the freshly completed terraced houses on a shared manning basis. The lower priced houses in the terrace prompted a fair amount of interest, though not approaching Woodbridge or Saxmundham levels, but after three weeks the number of callers no longer justified the sales office. Normal advertising continued in the local papers and a second agent was appointed to work in tandem with the first. Asking prices, edging downwards in a weak market, were periodically reviewed by the council's agents and the district valuer. By the end of the year, five of the properties had been found purchasers, but all were dependent on sales of other properties and no purchase was yet completed.

January 1983 saw the start of the public enquiry into the CEGB proposal to construct a second nuclear power station at Sizewell, 2 miles from Leiston. The proposal received wide media coverage. The purchaser nearest to exchange of contracts immediately withdrew, soon followed by another. Three of the five sales survived the opening hearings of the Sizewell enquiry, the start of a long period of uncertainty for Leiston. To add to Leiston's problems, the already limited work-force still employed at the former Garrett premises was further reduced, and soon one of the two firms then operating closed its doors. The award to High Green of a Europa Nostra Diploma in 1982 gave welcome cheer, and the long process of sales completion eventually bore fruit when, in spring 1983, the first two purchasers moved in, fol-lowed by others later in the year.

With the start in August 1983 of a Manpower Services Commission project at the museum, the Long Shop work quickened in pace and optimism, and plans were prepared for a formal opening in April 1984. Some of the new High Green residents became keen museum suppor-ters and took part in the second excuse in four years for a Leiston celebration when on Saturday 28 April, accompanied by the Leiston Band, the full regalia of working steam engines and with about one thousand onlookers, the museum was opened by HM Lord Lieutenant for Suffolk. From hesitant beginnings, the Long Shop Museum was on its way to becoming a source of growing interest to Leiston's residents and a tourist attraction to visitors, assisted by grants from the Manifold Trust, Pilgrim Trust, the Baring Foundation, the Scarfe Charitable Trust[6] and from the Historic Buildings Council and the district and town councils.

But it was not until early 1985 that all ten of the High Green houses were finally sold and occupied. From the point of view of turnover of capital, the project had been as disappointing as New Street and Angel Yard had been successful. The district council's revolving fund had been crippled by the interest charges on the capital tied up in the slow-selling houses. Even though it was part of a scheme embracing 2 acres of redundant Town Works buildings, the concept was inadequate to deal with Leiston's wider misfortunes. The package of joint charitable trust/private/public action that produced the museum, the surgery/clinic and High Green was not substantial enough in the short term to overcome the town's adverse economic and environmental climate. In the longer term, Leiston has a prize that should grow in fascination and value.

The Suffolk revolving fund dramatically, almost heroically, illustrates the ups, downs and risks that are part and parcel of the trade. It had the benefit of a flying start aided by exceptionally favourable market conditions, and it experienced an unequal fight against exceptionally adverse economic and social forces. Its schemes spanned the full range of small Suffolk towns in terms of their market popularity. Like all similar projects, it provided employment for a skilled labour force and encouragement for others to go ahead with their own schemes. It attracted attention from a wide area and a crop of national awards that reflected well on the council and helped to lift morale in the later becalmed stages of the Leiston scheme. Throughout it was staunchly defended by the two members of the council most closely involved, Councillors Grace Agate and Sidney Forton, who took turns to occupy the chair of the planning committee during the period of the three projects and who were required to satisfy the questions of less committed members.

Reflecting the spread of publicity, only half of the purchasers were from Suffolk — the others came from London (four), Surrey (three), Essex (two) and one each from Kent, Manchester, Norfolk, Belgium and West Germany. Middle-aged, professional purchasers were in the majority, some already retired, others looking forward to retirement and the convenience of town-centre living with daily necessities within easy reach and neighbours within easy call. Reducing the age imbalance, two younger households at New Street and Angel Yard each increased their family sizes not long after occupation!

The success of its first two schemes, roughly trebling the capital in the fund, eased but did not eliminate financial pressures later on. Although, with the benefit of hindsight, the outcome of the earlier projects suggests that they might equally have been carried out by voluntary groups, the Leiston scheme, with interest charges on £200,000 or

50

more of working capital over several years and nothing in return, might have annihilated the slender resources of a voluntary group well before completion. Even if it was considered to be a suitable project on which to make a loan in the first place, a commercial concern, with no sales in sight, might well have withdrawn support by the halfway stage. Delay would have increased dilapidation, and therefore the costs of reinstatement, and would have placed a questionmark against the prospects for a successful museum project on the adjoining, overlooking, site.

A community of ten households is now established in the formerly empty and dilapidated buildings that for years disfigured part of the centre of Leiston. It is turning houses into homes. Already it is active in local affairs, education, music, nature conservation, and when the museum needs some extra hands for a special event it knows it can rely on support, virtually *in situ*. None of this appears in the final balance sheet — it is a benefit that cannot be valued.

2
CITIES

Bristol

As befits a regional capital with nearly half a million inhabitants, Bristol has something of everything — medieval and Georgian quarters, a cathedral and university, a bustling docks, the famous suspension bridge built at Clifton by Brunel in 1864, a Georgian theatre and St Mary Redcliffe, said to have been described by Queen Elizabeth I as 'the fairest, goodliest and most famous parish church in the kingdom'. Bristol is still thought to resemble the London of a century ago.[1]

But in the early 1970s, beneath the tourist literature's cosy image of the city, hundreds of listed buildings were under threat and historic buildings were going down like ninepins, according to Dorothy Brown, chairman of the Bristol Visual and Environmental Buildings Trust. The trust is the buildings-repair offshoot of the slightly less wordy Bristol Visual and Environmental Group, set up in 1971 to bring to wide public notice the need — continuing but particularly pressing at that time — to prevent further damage to the city heritage. Concern by voluntary groups for the preservation of the history and the environment of Bristol is long-standing, and it has prompted the formation of several organisations with overlapping areas of interest. One of the city's earliest civic societies was formed in 1905 and remains active. Long before that the Bristol Municipal Charities was set up with broader social objectives, to manage the medieval charities concerned with housing the old and educating the young. In recent years the Bristol Engineering Centre Trust was formed to secure the restoration of Brunel's internationally known Temple Meads station, and the city council has sponsored a Buildings Preservation Trust, run by the council but with amenity societies represented on it. This was formed in 1981 and it preceded by one year the setting up of its own trust by the Environmental Group.

The Municipal Charities, the city-administered Buildings Preservation Trust and the Environmental Group and its trust were all involved in the efforts to save a property just off the ring road that skirts the centre of the city, 38–39 Old Market Street. Central in a group of prop-

52

erties between 35–41 Old Market Street, the property was formerly shops with living accommodation above, owned by Bristol Municipal Charities. At the end of 1980, when the whole group was in an advanced state of decay, Municipal Charities enquired about the possibility of an Architectural Heritage Fund loan to help with rehabilitation. The street was a leftover from the post-war comprehensive redevelopment plans that guided the rebuilding of much of the central area, including the ring road that severs it from the main shopping and business area. Medieval in origin, Old Market Street had been designated a conserva- tion area and the properties in the group, 35–41, were listed. No 35 was in the worst state of all and was scheduled for demolition. The DoE had refused permission for demolition of the rest: they formed the most sig- nificant group of seventeenth- and early eighteenth-century properties remaining in the street, so had acquired scarcity value, and were con- sidered eminently worth preserving. On land behind Old Market Street, proposals for development, which could have the effect of upgrading the area and raising the value of the old buildings, were under consideration by a progeny of Bristol Municipal Charities, the Orchard Housing Association.

Although the AHF expressed interest, Bristol Municipal Charities later withdrew its application for loan assistance. The city council's Buildings Preservation Trust then contemplated taking on the proper- ties for its own first project but the final outcome was that Municipal Charities decided to renovate Nos 36–37 themselves, to sell Nos 40–41 to a private restoring purchaser who was already repairing No 42, and to sell Nos 38–39 to the Bristol Visual and Environmental Group whose members had been the first, back in 1971, to lobby for the preservation of the Old Market Street buildings. At the rear the housing association development was confirmed and, with the city council as co-ordinator, details of access, parking and landscaping were jointly agreed for the whole group.

To tackle their part of the scheme, the Environmental Group set up Bristol Visual and Environmental Buildings Trust Ltd. Its instigator and secretary describes herself as a former housewife turned builder, evidently someone with a practical approach. Also on its executive committee are two solicitors, a retired accountant, a magistrate, a housewife-cum-farmer, a teacher and a retired university lecturer. A feasibility study financed by the city council and Municipal Charities had decided that the buildings, fronting a main road, were unsuitable for housing and the trust reluctantly agreed, deciding to renovate Nos 38–39 as showrooms on the ground floor and offices on the two floors above.

Finance came from a wide variety of sources: the AHF offered a loan of £40,000 towards the total estimated cost of £117,000; a HBC grant of over £36,000; a borrowing facility negotiated with Barclays Bank of up to £20,000 at 1½ per cent over base rate; bridging loans from individual members of the Trust totalling £20,000; a local charity, Richard Davies Charitable Foundation, made a loan of £10,000; grants from the city council towards repair work and road and paving works; and a £7,000 donation from the group itself.

Renovation work started in August 1982 and was completed in October 1983. The trust decided not to spend too much on advertising until the buildings on each side, several months behind the trust's schedule, were more or less finished, although photographs did appear in the local evening paper at the time of completion. The paper also covered the formal opening six months later in March 1984, when eighty guests were invited, along with the local MP, William Waldegrave, a minister at the DoE, who had helped to resolve a problem with the related housing association programme affecting the backland and access to both schemes.

In October 1984 a computer company, introduced via a selling agent, purchased a 999 year lease on Nos 38–39. The lease included conditions covering insurance and maintenance and the trust retained power to take remedial action if the property became neglected. The terms of the lease produced about a £20,000 profit for the trust, but much of this would not have occurred without interest-free loans, low management and professional fees arising out of goodwill towards the trust and voluntary work by its members.

The visual result of this joint effort is the striking transformation of a major part of Old Market Street with the half-hipped gable end of Nos 38–39 in its centre. The renovation shows admirable restraint: if the trust was at any stage tempted to complete the symmetry of the gable the temptation was quite properly resisted. Without the refurbishment of the adjoining properties, the scheme would have been less successful visually and commercially. Many hours of painstaking discussions and negotiations must have been put in by all the parties involved to carry through a scheme of this complexity, a difficult but immensely rewarding exercise on which the trust could cut its teeth.

Plates 12 and 13 (Suffolk) The Leiston scheme, seen here before and after renovation, is loosely grouped around an open space after which High Green takes its name. The Works House is on the right *(Suffolk Coastal District Council* and *Edward Morgan)*

Not of a mind to sit back with self-satisfaction upon completion of the sale, the trust immediately bought for renovation Acton Court, an important Grade II* fourteenth- to sixteenth-century manor house 11 miles outside the city. It is in a ruinous state, but with the trust as its owner, this should soon be changed. However, the trust is already finding it much more difficult to get things moving on its own, as it were, compared with working under the protective aura of the city council.

Meanwhile, the city-sponsored building preservation trust, having decided against taking on 38–39 Old Market Street, partly because of the ability of the Environmental Buildings Trust to do so and partly on cost grounds, has undertaken its own first project at 72 and 74 Colston Street. Its board of management consists of ten councillors and five members of various local amenity societies. It is advised and administered by the city council, which donated working capital of £50,000, but it hopes to double this with private contributions which are invited by an attractive appeal leaflet. The Bristol Buildings Preservation Trust sees its main purposes as:

1 Investigating why properties, individually or in groups, are derelict.
2 Promoting their repair by others or, if nobody else is willing, purchasing, restoring and reselling them itself.

The trust calculated that in the late 1970s, alongside the massive investment in the redevelopment of Bristol's central area, there was a staggering total of 470 vacant or derelict historic buildings in the inner area of the city. Many having been blighted by unfulfilled plans for comprehensive redevelopment, only about half have been restored, and the restoration by the city trust of 72 and 74 Colston Street as flats and small shops will complete the work on an extensive frontage of that street.[2] The trust is also assisting in the management of a joint council/DoE conservation programme for the inner city.

In addition to the Old Market Street and Colston Street schemes, work by two more charities is now in hand: the former Jacob Wells Baths, a listed building in the Clifton conservation area, is being converted by the Bristol Dance Centre, an educational charity, into what it intends to be the centre of dance for the West of England;[3] and, with

Plates 14 and 15 (above) A Victorian fire engine was part of the Long Shop Museum's display when the refurbished Works House at Leiston was formally opened by the Duke of Gloucester on 17 July 1981. *(below)* This was an occasion that gave pleasure to Leiston people of all ages *(Suffolk Coastal District Council* and *East Anglian Daily Times)*

even higher ambitions, the Brunel Engineering Centre Trust is embarked on a £4 million scheme to adapt Brunel's Temple Meads station as a national centre for engineering.[4] Both projects are supported by the AHF. The Bristol tradition of action by voluntary groups in areas of educational and environmental concern seems to be gaining ground after the setbacks of the 1950s and '60s.

Derby

Crown Derby porcelain, Rolls-Royce engines and railway workshops are all closely associated with Derby, and it is largely around these industries that the city, a status bestowed by Queen Elizabeth II in her Silver Jubilee year, has developed in modern times. Now with a population of more than 200,000, Derby, although having Roman origins, only began to make significant growth during the Industrial Revolution when the Midland Railway built huge workshops in the town, and it became known as a major centre for railway engineering. So it is the town's comparatively recent development that more than anything creates Derby's personality, Victorian and modern, businesslike and enterprising. With the passing of time the Victorian element has acquired historical interest and value.

It should therefore have come as no surprise that the Derby Civic Society, set up in 1960 for the specific purpose of helping to retain the best of the town's historical and architectural features, viewed with dismay the 1978 proposals by the city council to demolish a key part of Derby's legacy — a group of fifty-seven houses standing opposite the Midland Railway's headquarters station and built by the company in 1841–2 for its employees. Apart from their architectural merit, they were an outstanding example of early Victorian industrial town planning for, in addition to the houses, there were originally a corner shop and an inn, something of a village in its own right.

The city council had bought the properties from British Rail for demolition because they stood in the path of a relief road and, although in 1978 most were still occupied, they were in a sufficiently run-down state for the council to consider it impractical to bring them up to acceptable modern standards. The Civic Society had other ideas: it produced a feasibility study for the area, showing how the council could divert the planned relief road, saving the houses so that they could be renovated. The feasibility study attracted the interest of the Derbyshire Historic Buildings Trust, which in turn brought it to the the attention of national conservation bodies. Together, the trust and the Civic Society persuaded a city council big enough to change its mind to accept the trust's plans to undertake extensive environmental improvements, realign the main road, purchase the houses, renovate and then resell them on the open market. This was in an area planned to be non-residential and unfit for habitation.

The Derbyshire Historic Buildings Trust, a registered charity devoted to the preservation of the county's environment and heritage, was established in 1974 as a result of the European Architectural Heritage Year campaign. It sprang from a county council initiative and is chaired by a management consultant who at that time was also a county councillor. By the time it purchased the railway houses in 1979, the trust, starting with an initial capital of less than £5,000, had several schemes already completed or under way on a revolving-fund basis. Its first project, begun in Heritage Year and completed a year later was a mid-nineteenth-century turnpike cottage under threat of demolition by the county council on the edge of Derby. Because of its small size and its proximity to the main road, many people thought it would be difficult to sell, but in the event it sold easily and the trust made a 14 per cent profit. Similar fears about saleability were voiced about a much larger project, the renovation of two rows of eighteenth- and nineteenth-century canal-side cottages built by the Butterley Ironworks for their employees at Golden Valley, near Ripley.[1] Here the total capital involved was £250,000.

The properties were in the district council's clearance programme, an application by the council to rehabilitate them having been refused by the DoE. By means of the revolving principle, the maximum cash flow requirement at any one time was reduced to £120,000, and this was raised by a combination of historic building grants, improvement grants, a loan from the AHF and a contribution from the trust's own capital fund. The twenty stone cottages, built in 1797, were fully renovated to form eleven larger cottages, but the later ones of brick construction were only supplied with basic services, given an external facelift and sold, within two weeks of completion, to 'self-help' owners. Other projects that helped the trust to build up a useful background of experience before it took on the railway cottages included a stone farmhouse, again threatened by the local council's slum clearance programme, and a completely derelict and vandalised Church of England school which the trust converted into a house whilst keeping the external appearance intact.

Even so, the renovation of fifty-seven houses incorporating seventeen different house types at an estimated cost of £1.25 million broke new ground, both in its size and in the preliminaries that were needed on the part of the authorities before building work could start. A clearance order was rescinded, the land use zoning was changed from industrial to residential (who would buy a house in an area zoned for industry?), the route of the new road was changed, a conservation area designated and a general improvement area declared, which led directly to the offer of a £43,000 GIA grant from the city council towards general environmental improvements. Permission was given for the closure of the roads on two sides of the triangle to form a cul-de-sac. The realignment of a busy road away from the houses provided space for small gardens at the front as well as at the rear. All these vital steps relied on the full support of the city council. Finally, the houses were included by the DoE in the statutory list of buildings of architectural or historic interest (Grade II).

In spite of all the paperwork, only three months after agreeing to purchase, the way was clear by late 1979 for fund raising for construction work. The AHF offered a loan of £250,000, the HBC offered a grant totalling £62,250 over three years and a generous loan facility was negotiated with the county council. This was sufficient to enable the work to proceed, which it did on 12 August 1980 when the Provost of Derby Cathedral removed the first patch of grime from one of the gable ends. Within two years the work was complete. The trust estimates that the cost of the restoration to full modern standards is equivalent to the cost of new houses of the same area.

The properties vary in size from two-bedroom cottages to four-bedroom houses. Some have parking space in front, others use a parking court. In the centre of the site there is a quiet communal sitting area. The external colour is that of the original Midland Railway scheme, and purchasers are covenanted to keep to this under the terms of their purchase. A maintenance manual is given to purchasers, setting out their rights and responsibilities and giving practical advice about upkeep.

Prearranged by the trust, several building societies agreed to make mortgage facilities available, show houses were opened and television cameras recorded queues of purchasers outside the agents' office as each batch of properties was completed and put on the market. A formal opening, part of the trust's policy in each of its schemes, helped to give valuable additional publicity. The publicity was so successful that when the second batch of properties was released for sale, prospective purchasers camped on the pavement all night outside the agents' office.

As in the Golden Valley scheme, the finance came from a variety of sources:

Loans	Architectural Heritage Fund	£250,000
	Midland Bank	£125,000
	County Council	£ 25,000
Grants	City Council (improvement grant)	£184,000
	Historic Buildings Council	£ 62,250
	City Council (GIA grant)	£ 43,000
	County Council (historic buildings)	£ 30,000
	City Council (historic buildings)	£ 15,000
Trust capital	approximately	£300,000

Extensive negotiations, running into over a hundred meetings, were required to resolve health, grant, highway, general improvement area, drainage, water, statutory undertakers' and structural requirements.

The Derbyshire Historic Buildings Trust has carried out over thirty schemes. It has a council of management of thirty, drawn from local authorities and amenity societies and including some private individuals. The council has overall control but it delegates extensively to its chairman and to a technical panel which includes architects, engineers, surveyors and valuers in private practice and in local government. The panel considers on-the-spot appraisals from small working parties on buildings at risk and makes recommendations for acquisition to the trust council. The trust has:

1 A well-established working group of about five people who have the support of many more.
2 The ability to make quick decisions on purchase.
3 Built up expertise and confidence, starting cautiously in its choice of schemes and gradually becoming more ambitious.
4 Been ready to support local authorities considering serving a repairs notice by offering, if necessary, to purchase from the authority the property concerned.
5 Recognised the importance of marketing, such as the television cameras at the railway cottages agents' office.
6 Paid the full rate for the job — it is considered by the trust that a voluntary or cheap job is usually at the bottom of the in-tray.
7 The capacity, through its technical adviser, to see the hidden potential as well as the problems of restoration.
8 Knowledge of grant and loan sources and procedures.
9 Enlisted the help of sympathetic estate agents, but still been prepared to back its own judgement where an agent has difficulty in visualising the proposal.
10 Established helpful contacts in the local authorities.

In 1978 it had seemed likely that the railway houses in Derby would be demolished. It only needed events to take their normal course for this to have happened, with the loss of housing conveniently located within

61

¾ mile of the city centre. Even if it had been replaced by new housing, the density of the replacement would probably have been lower. Demolition would also have meant the loss of part of Derby's irreplaceable heritage. Since the cost of the restoration is similar to that of new houses, the historic interest and architectural appeal is a bonus from which the city and the purchasers benefit. More recently, the pub that was a key element in the original Victorian complex has also been restored. In the early stages the timely intervention of the civic society and its allies and the persuasive feasibility study were crucial, as was the willingness of the city council to look at alternative ideas to its own.

Edinburgh

Dereliction is not what first springs to mind in the context of noble Edinburgh, one of Europe's most impressive capitals, rich in history and abundantly endowed with memorable buildings. In Princes Street, as well as the great crag-perched castle, the visitor will see attractive gardens, busy prosperous shops and, only a few steps away, the elegant Georgian streets and squares of James Craig's New Town. Tourism is big business. Visitors staying in Edinburgh in 1976 are calculated to have spent over £17 million[1] and it is reasonable to attribute a major part of this income to the attraction of the city's historic buildings. A survey of summer visitors to Edinburgh carried out by the University of Edinburgh in 1971 on behalf of the Scottish Tourist Board found that the main reasons for coming to Edinburgh were its history and old buildings. Visitors tend to spend heavily in hotels, shops, transport services and entertainment — all labour-intensive industries, so expenditure on conserving its built history is a sensible business investment of general benefit to the city, as well as being architecturally satisfying.

Yet ever since it was first published in 1972, the pages of the Cockburn Association's regular newsletter have been full of sad stories of neglected historic properties, partly no doubt because Edinburgh has one of the highest concentrations of historic buildings of any city in Britain. The Cockburn Association is Edinburgh's Civic Trust, and for over one hundred years it had been campaigning for the restoration of old buildings and urging others to restore them when, in 1978, the association launched the Cockburn Conservation Trust to enable its members to participate in restoration schemes themselves and set an example of how this should be done. The trust, taking its cue from the pioneering work of the National Trust for Scotland, was established to acquire, restore and sell dilapidated but interesting old buildings in Edinburgh on the revolving-fund principle. It is a limited company with charitable status, technically independent of the Cockburn Association, but its directors are all association members and it is administered by the association's staff, a full-time secretary and a part-time assistant secretary working from a small office in the centre of the city.

In addition to its established organisation and membership, the Cockburn Conservation Trust started life with a number of other advantages: an option on two potentially most attractive buildings; the full backing of the city district council, whose estates surveyor was helpful in making appropriate properties owned by the council available to the trust on favourable terms; firm links with Edinburgh's business and professional community; and the promise of support from the Civic Trust's Architectural Heritage Fund. Newsletter No 19 in December 1978 announced that, as well as commercial firms and other charitable trusts, the trust was looking to Cockburn members for about 50 per cent of the cost of the proposed work that was needed, either in the form of donations or interest-free loans. 'Two important conservation projects already under way — now is your chance to help us prove that unloved old buildings in Edinburgh can be brought back to life — at a profit,' was the clarion call in the trust's well-presented appeal leaflet.

The trust moved swiftly and a little over a year later (February 1980) it could look back on its first scheme — four flats and three shops in Candlemaker Row completed and, just as important, sold. This remarkable demonstration of practical conservation was largely due to the success of the appeal which, in the short time since the trust was launched, had raised £28,500, made up of £10,500 in donations and the remainder in interest-free loans. Scottish Gas contributed the entire cost of one central heating installation.[2] The response to the appeal meant that the contract on Candlemaker Row was well advanced before the trust had to take up the loan for the part of the cost not covered by the appeal. In the event it was found that a commercial loan from the Royal Bank of Scotland was even more advantageous than the terms offered by the AHF, though the latter's existence and early promise of support was of critical importance when the Cockburn Conservation Trust was founded.

The first two schemes were the renovation of buildings previously in council ownership, but given to the trust on the basis of a 50/50 split of any profit. Nos 46–54 Candlemaker Row, on the fringe of the old town, dated from about 1720 and were formerly two shops on the ground and first floors with a labyrinth of rooms above used as a karate club. The trust's architects produced a conversion into three shops and four two-bedroomed flats. A leading firm of Edinburgh estate agents advised that there should be no difficulty in selling the shops and flats at a total price which ought to show a handsome surplus. Starting in March 1979, the Lord Provost performed an opening ceremony in the autumn and the work was completed in November. The association newsletter reported:

> Eleven months after the contractors' work began, two of the flats are occupied and other new owners will soon be moving in. The Trust's first customers are apparently delighted with their new homes and there has been much praise, from owners and numerous visitors, for the high quality of the largely new flat interiors; it is not every new house that has cornices in all main rooms, panelled doors throughout, brass door furniture, and a polished mahogany handrail on the stair! These details, as well as more conventional features and the character and location of the buildings, ensured that there was great interest in the properties, and a substantial surplus on the contract.

With its capital recouped, the way was open for the second project — Nos 16–18 Calton Hill, a few steps from the City Observatory and Waterloo Place at the east end of Princes Street. It was once part of a larger terrace built in the 1770s but the lower half had been demolished as part of the St James shopping centre and Eastern link road schemes, a standard piece of 1960s planning which left the mutilated terrace standing untidily at the end of a temporary footbridge. The lowest remaining building, Nos 16–18, had long been empty and at first sight seemed to have little architectural merit — a square, rendered and unlisted box — but the box shape concealed what originally had been a far more interesting gabled structure. The trust set out to restore the pitched roof and reveal the gables, providing in the process one two-bedroomed and three three-bedroomed flats with a shared paved and planted area in front and a garden for the basement flat at the rear.

In order to terminate the terrace in a satisfactory manner, the trust considered that it was desirable to reconstruct a building on the site of No 14, but, even if it had the resources, the trust had been unable to persuade the Inland Revenue that it should have the power to construct new buildings as part of conservation schemes. Instead, it was agreed that a housing association would take over plans by the trust's architects for the new building, which would be constructed as part of a concurrent contract with Nos 16 and 18. Work began in the spring of 1981 and was completed by late autumn. The four flats were opened on 20 November of that year by the Minister of State for the Environment, who gave the buildings listed status. By rescuing this eighteenth-century tenement from its mutilated state, the trust had created a 'new'

Figs 2 and 3 No 16–18 Calton Hill, Edinburgh, lacked any aesthetic appeal until they were rescued by the Cockburn Conservation Trust. Soon afterwards their merit was recognised by inclusion in the statutory list of buildings of architectural or historic interest

building of architectural or historic interest. The following day the scheme was open for general public inspection and furniture, on loan from a local antique shop, added distinction to No 16.

Two of the flats were sold within a month of the opening, but with occupation not until the end of January, the building was vacant over the holiday period. The central heating system had been left on as a frost precaution and to help dry out new plaster, but unfortunately the boiler in the top flat burst, resulting in several days' undetected flooding in all four flats. Once ownership and insurance problems had been resolved, the trust carried out repairs and the two remaining flats were soon sold, but repair costs were considerable — only partly covered by insurance — and the project just covered its costs.

The final total audited cost for the Candlemaker Row and Calton Hill projects came to £264,943. The surplus arising from the sale prices was £36,068, mostly from Candlemaker Row. Taken with the visual improvement in the two streets, this must have been regarded as an eminently satisfactory outcome by all those who had supported the trust. Meanwhile, a third project was being pursued — 1, 2 and 3 Glanville Place, Stockbridge — about ¼ mile outside James Craig's New Town but still, in the early nineteenth century, part of Edinburgh's late Georgian inheritance. The building was the subject of a dangerous structures notice so the trust first commissioned an engineer's report and then architect's plans in partnership with the proprietors of the two ground-floor shops. Above the shops are six flats on three floors. Part had been empty for over ten years, foundations were inadequate, cracks in the outside walls were obvious and the internal walls were not very well tied to the main structure. The district council's Director of Building Control, who had been responsible for serving the dangerous structures notice, showed considerable patience as the trust tried to disentangle flat-ownership difficulties. Four of the six were offered to the trust for a nominal sum, but the title to one was held by a woman of whom there had been no record since she left for Australia in 1905.

In spite of the complications, the purchase and the work eventually proceeded, enabling structural and external works to start in April 1982, dove-tailing neatly with the completion of the sales in Calton Hill, followed by the fitting out of the six flats, three with two bedrooms and three with one bedroom.

Having demonstrated its practical abilities in the best way possible, the trust is keen to increase its scale of operations. It believes that a full working partnership with the district council might be of mutual benefit. The combination of the trust's charitable status and ability to raise cheap finance with the council's statutory authority and resources would, it is believed, make both organisations better equipped to carry out a programme of work on the scale required. Possibilities include the appointment of a district council director on the trust's management committee and the return of renovated properties to the council for local authority housing. There is still plenty to be done.

London, Southwark

The dome of St Paul's and the four pinnacles of the fifteenth-century tower of Southwark Cathedral can both be seen from the River Thames but, except for their common urban qualities, there is little else shared by those areas of London north and south of the river, in which the two cathedrals stand.

Three generations of the Kirkaldy family worked in Southwark as testers of engineering and building materials. David Kirkaldy (1820–97) started the business, which in 1874 he transferred to a purpose-built building at 99 Southwark Street, where the new testing works quickly established an international reputation. The original testing machine, nearly 50ft long, was able to apply a load of over 300 tons and was used, amongst other things, to test parts of the Tay bridge after the 1879 disaster. Any material could be tested to destruction, establishing precisely the pressure it could withstand. Consulting engineers, contractors, shipbuilders, boilermakers, steelmakers, railway companies, engineering institutions, insurance companies and government bodies all made use of David Kirkaldy's giant testing machine. The motto

Fig 4 'Facts Not Opinions': the motto over the door of Kirkcaldy's Testing Works at 99 Southwark Street, London

above the main entrance door reads 'Facts not opinions', and for over ninety years, until 1965, the facts were in demand.

From 1974 until 1982 Kirkaldy's Testing Works stood empty. Then the Industrial Buildings Preservation Trust, established in 1975 for the preservation of just such buildings as Kirkaldy's, acquired the freehold from the Crown Commissioners and started the major task of refurbishing the building and its contents — the testing machine was still in position, dusty and unused but intact. Potential buyers may have been deterred by the wish of the Crown Commissioners that the machinery be preserved, but the preservation trust were encouraged by a GLC-funded feasibility study by Nicholas Falk of Urban and Economic Developments Ltd (URBED), which showed that a range of buildings in Southwark Street, Nos 93–99, had possibilities for economic reuse. The feasibility study drew on work by the architects Duffy, Eley, Giffone, Worthington which showed how the various regulations could be satisfied by a mixed-use scheme, and followed appraisals by Bernard Williams Associates (surveyors) which established the economic viability of the scheme. Both firms subsequently helped the trust with implementation.

The joint Trust/Falk plan was for the lower two floors to house a Kirkaldy Testing Museum, featuring the preserved and renovated testing machine, and to adapt the upper three floors into 6,000 sq ft of mainly office lettable workspace, suitable for small or young growing firms. To develop and administer the museum the Kirkaldy Testing Museum, Southwark, was formed and given a twenty-five-year lease at a peppercorn rent. An organisation of Friends of the Museum[1] was set up to provide voluntary help in maintaining and operating the machinery.

Commercially, Kirkaldy's has the advantage of a central location. It is within walking distance of three main railway stations and just across the river from the City of London. Carpeted office and studio space, from as little as 100 sq ft, is available on 'easy-in, easy-out' licences. Meeting rooms are bookable by the hour, enabling firms to keep overheads to a minimum. Businesses from out of London can take desk space and use Kirkaldy's as a business base. There are also some self-contained light industrial units. An electronic door entry system provides security with twenty-four-hour access, seven days a week. Typing, word processing, photocopying, report production and message-taking services are shared. The telephone system is also shared and provides for messages to be taken and for bills to be individually monitored. Since the building is owned by the Industrial Buildings Preservation Trust, a registered charity, rents are kept to the minimum. The 1984 rent or licence fee was from £175 a month for a one-man business and covers heating, lighting, cleaning, insurance, reception, telephone system and building management.

Before it acquired Kirkaldy's, the trust had completed projects in Rotherhithe in London's dockland, where it converted a group of riverside warehouses into craft workshops, a community arts centre and a community workshop with funding from the local authority, charitable foundations and bank loans.

Kirkaldy's structure was, of necessity, strong to support the heavy machinery it contained in the basement and on the ground floor and, although it had been unoccupied for eight years, the property was in sound condition when the trust acquired it. The distinctive brick façade to Southwark Street has an appropriately powerful look, and the trust and its architects realised that if it were cleaned it would make a strong and attractive impression on the street scene. The cleaning of the façade and the conversion of the three upper floors to bring in an income were the first priorities. The museum organisation, set up and led by Dr Denis Smith, chairman of the GLC Industrial Archaeology Society, took on the lower floors. Thanks to the generosity of David Kirkaldy's grandson and the efforts of the Friends, the testing machine has been restored to working order.

URBED was the third partner in the project. Since 1976 it has been widely involved in helping to turn what to some may have appeared pipe-dreams into practical projects. It has done this by joining up two sometimes unconnected ends of the development process: the building or environmental, and the employment and potential needs of the area concerned. So as well as undertaking studies on inner-city regeneration, acting as consultants on projects involving wasteland and buildings, and raising finance for complex development schemes, URBED has run training programmes to help people start new businesses, advised organisations, large as well as small, on how to launch new ventures and offered a range of business services to enable small firms to start and, hopefully, grow. These activities are now all run from URBED's new base at Kirkaldy's. It is an independent non-profit-making company, profits being ploughed back into research and development. On 3 May 1984 the refurbished Kirkaldy's was opened by Hamish Orr-Ewing, chairman of Rank Xerox, who had helped in the creation of the museum. The total cost of the scheme was £253,000, including £35,000 for the purchase of the building and £5,000 for VAT. Finance came in the form of a £70,000 loan from the AHF, guaranteed by the National Westminster Bank, a £70,000 Inner Urban Areas improvement grant obtained through the London Borough of South-wark, a £53,000 grant from the GLC and a bank overdraft. Fully let, the building has been valued at £300,000.

As well as URBED, occupiers of the upper floors include a catering firm, graphic designers and printers, a computer software bureau, building services engineers, a billiard-cue maker and the office services firm which provides message-taking and other services for the firms in the building. Nicholas Falk arranged for the neighbouring end of the block studied in his GLC report to be bought by a developer who has turned it into flats, and Falk points to at least ten other old buildings in the area which have been or are now being refurbished since the Kirkaldy's project began in 1982.

Kirkaldy's is but one of many successful examples of the reuse of supposedly redundant industrial buildings. In London alone there are estimated to be over 30 million sq ft of unused industrial floor space, and Falk sees the main problem now as being the pace of rehabilitation. To quicken this up he suggests five main steps. The first is to take stock of all the empty space in the area concerned. The second, by means of feasibility studies,[2] to select the most promising possibilities and pro-vide information for negotiating with property owners and funding agencies. The third step is a concerted effort to solve the environmental and access problems of areas with high levels of vacant space, using an approach in which all interests collaborate. In this work, non-profit-making building, historical and environmental trusts can have a valuable role to play as they may be able to provide assistance on a voluntary basis in the crucial early stages. Their strong commitment to improve the neighbourhood, along with low overheads, can also attract public and private resources, and they may be able to undertake more com-plex schemes than private investors would normally bother with.

The fourth step is to involve local professional and community groups, looking for work or accommodation. They can help with the planning and building phase and, as in Kirkaldy's, even become tenants in the completed scheme. Finally, perhaps the most important of all, is the need to win over the institutions so as to ensure that the reuse pro-cess is not halted through lack of funds. To attract institutional finance, Falk believes it may be necessary to involve, or set up more financial intermediaries, like URBED which can take on in a convincing profes-sional manner the role of assessing whether schemes are worth backing and provide the detailed management.

Similar steps shaped the renovation at Kirkaldy's and turned a daunting task into a viable one — that is not an opinion, it is a fact!

London, Spitalfields

The Spital Fields were green until the end of the seventeenth century, when the Huguenot silk weavers, refugees from the Revocation of the Edict of Nantes in 1685, settled in the area. The Huguenots arrived as a working community, and soon the fields became streets made up of elegant houses to live and work in and chapels in which to worship. It was in the 1720s that much of the Georgian architecture was built, including mighty Christ Church, Nicholas Hawksmoor's grandest church, started in 1723 and completed only six years later. This was the period of Spitalfields' greatest prosperity, but when the silk trade stagnated whole families of poor workers from the city moved into single rooms of the homes of the rich who had left. Starting in the late eighteenth century, throughout the nineteenth and much of the twentieth century, the poverty seemed bottomless. The little money available was spent on the necessities for survival, and the buildings were left to look after themselves.

A sharp-eyed observer of people and places in the 1960s, Ian Nairn, wrote in *Nairn's London*:

> It [Spitalfields] went down as the East End grew up, and the big taciturn brick houses are now on their last legs: ironically it is the biggest area of its date left in London. Elder Street and Wilkes Street have hardly altered since 1750; unexpected treasure turns up, like the Great Synagogue in Fournier Street and the Georgian shopfront at 56 Artillery Lane — easily the best in London, with gusto as well as polish, now used as a storeroom. The whole area seems bound to go, not only because rehabilitation would be difficult, but quite simply because nobody loves it. Christ Church looms over the whole area, the meths drinkers lie around nearby: charity is far enough away and compassion even further. For tourists who visit the cheerful market at Petticoat Lane (Middlesex Street) on Sunday mornings, this sombre ghost is just beyond. It could even now be one of those living areas in the heart of cities over which so many pious words are spilt at conferences.

This has the authentic, helpless, pessimism of the time it was written, but the author lived to see Spitalfields, in spite of the momentum of two centuries of decline, on its way to becoming the living area he wished for.

Pious words are not the stock-in-trade of the Spitalfields Trust. With a nucleus of architectural historians and journalists, fully aware of the rich potential and determined to reverse its decline, the trust was founded in 1977 to acquire, renovate and resell historic buildings, and to agitate to prevent their destruction. Few areas can have had greater need for such an organisation. Of the 240 buildings listed as being of

CITIES

architectural or historic interest in 1957, no less than 90 had been demolished twenty years later, and 9 more were under immediate threat.

On the positive side, the trust saw some offsetting advantages. The same deprivation that had afflicted the area for so long meant that the houses had been less altered than most of their period and much original interior detail survived, a useful bonus alongside the intrinsic dignity of the early Georgian streets and doorways. The same streets were dominated by Hawksmoor's powerful gem, Christ Church. The intensive activity of the city lay only a few steps away and the whole area, with one of the capital's railheads on its doorstep, was one of the most easily accessible of any in London.

Nos 5 and 7 Elder Street were acquired in the trust's first year when the houses were in an advanced state of decay, and demolition — already making advances elsewhere in the street — had commenced. Nos 1 and 3 had been demolished following dangerous structures notices and 9 had structural problems. If 5 and 7 could not be saved, the whole eastern terrace was at risk. The position when the trust became involved was as follows: listed building consent to demolish had been granted; three dangerous structures notices had been served; the owner was seeking tenders for the demolition work; the sale of the cleared site to a housing trust had been agreed by the owner and the various authorities and a redevelopment scheme had been prepared. To prevent matters proceeding further along these lines, trust members occupied the houses in the summer of 1977, erected a tarpaulin roof and started negotiations with the owners and the housing trust. It also investigated the implications of the notices served on the buildings and the listed building consent to demolish.

Soon afterwards, demolition contractors entered the houses, removed the temporary roof and started dismantling the main walls. They were stopped on a technicality. Then, with assistance from the press, the trust was able to put considerable pressure on the owners. They eventually agreed to sell the houses provided that matters could be resolved with the housing trust. The amount of fees for abortive work required by the housing trust was substantial, but negotiations between the Housing Corporation and the HBC — two arms of government

Plates 16 and 17 Old Market Street, Bristol before *(above)* and after *(below)* renovation. The Bristol Visual and Environmental Trust's scheme, Nos 38–39 with the half-hipped gable, was part of a co-ordinated refurbishment involving several properties *(Bristol Visual and Environmental Buildings Trust)*

72

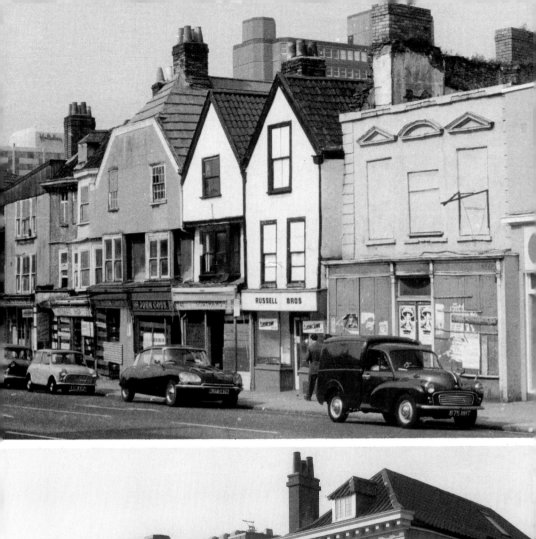

pulling, in this case, in different directions — eventually led to the corporation paying half the fees and to the HBC aiding the repairs with a substantial grant.

It was then vital for the trust to secure its new acquisition against collapse, first, by means of timber shores to the cross-walls between 3 and 5 and then by means of a scaffold tied into the front elevation. This met the requirements of the district surveyor's dangerous structures notice. The scaffold was then extended vertically to provide support for a temporary corrugated-iron roof, thereby allowing the structure to dry out slowly. Incoming services were disconnected and the building made safe against vagrants.

Internally the houses were a mess, stacked high with decaying furniture, plaster and rubbish while the basements were awash as a result of severed water mains, but once the building had been secured, a breathing space was obtained during which the rubbish was cleared and full repair and adaptation proposals were worked out. A building contract was let on a fixed-price basis with a bill of quantities, to a firm experienced in historic building repairs,

An illuminating account of the whole repair process and conservation philosophy through to completion was given by the trust itself in its supporting statement for 5 and 7 Elder Street in the RICS/Times Conservation Awards 1980:

> The first task concerned one of the most interesting features of the houses, an original leaded quarry-light window which was discovered half complete under layers of hardboard and felting. This window was in such a delicate state that it had to be removed entirely for conservation before reconstruction could start.
>
> Following a very detailed contour survey of the façades, unstable and fractured brickwork was taken down to the 2nd floor sill level of the front elevation and in an irregular pattern to the rear extensions, so reflecting the pattern of instability and decay.
>
> The part-framed floors were examined joist by joist, decayed joist ends were spliced or doubled, cracked joists were splinted and joints repegged. The wide boarding was relaid and renailed. After structural analysis a system of floor hangers and a basement prop was devised to reduce the deflection of the existing floor structures and thereby to remove stress from the collapsing staircase.

Plates 18 and 19 In their derelict state the Railway Cottages in Derby looked very unlike anyone's ideal home, but after they had received the imaginative attention of the Derbyshire Historic Buildings Trust people queued to buy them *(Derbyshire Historic Buildings Trust)*

Fig 5 The temporary scaffolded roof that was required in the early stages of the work at 5–7 Elder Street, Spitalfields was itself an impressive achievement

Once the floors were repaired and stiffened the outward leaning front and the 3/5 party walls were tied to them by means of non-ferrous straps and ties. This secured the basic shell of the buildings as taken over and established a secure foundation for the new stress calculated roofs. These firm new structures were then used to secure the new parapets and chimneys, built to their original profiles.

These works completed the primary consolidation of the buildings, paving the way for the laying of pantile roofs, the installation of services, the repair of staircases and panelling, as well as windows and doors. All the panelling and doors were repaired by an individual craftsman.

The client was particularly anxious to use secondhand handmade pantiles for the roofs as this was the tradition in the area. This presented certain problems which had to be overcome. Adequate quantities of secondhand pantiles can only be supplied if collected from several old stripped roofs. They are thus made up of tiles from different moulds which do not interlock in a very weather-proof manner. This problem was overcome by double-felting, cutting and a certain amount of sorting and nailing.

In order to retain as much material as possible the staircase was repaired one tread at a time with new nosings pieced in where necessary. The whole stair is constructed around a $3'' \times 3''$ newel about 40 feet in length and is scarfed out of three pieces of material, to which the treads and risers were merely spiked. Each tread had a half-bearer underneath to give additional support between newel and enclosing panelling. After repair by screwing and glueing, the underside was further reinforced by expanded metal lathing to form a basis for the plaster flewing.

Drawings were prepared of all panelling and of every door and window as a basis for determining the extent of repair. Wherever possible original material was retained by piecing in or reconstruction rather than replacement.

No attempt was made to reinstate the original wide glazing bars where sashes had to be replaced, as it was felt that this would have resulted in an arbitrary and random pattern which would have disrupted the regularity of the façade. If it had been necessary to replace all the sashes to the front façades consideration might have been given to the possibility of reinstating some earlier arrangement.

Kitchens were located in pleasant east-facing rooms at 1st floor, which retained original fireplaces and panelled cupboards but were without wall panelling. Internal bathrooms were inserted at 2nd floor, the space being formed by new panelled partitions.

The front doors were carefully repaired and the original ironmongery replaced after repair. New door hoods were constructed to a pattern found elsewhere in the street. The front areas were cleared, iron grilles overhauled and the stuccoed basement walls repaired and painted.

Internally, one room in each house has been decorated to its original colour scheme, as deduced from paint scrapes taken from doors and panelling. The remaining rooms have been decorated in simple light-reflective colours. Externally, the paint colours have been carefully chosen as an overall scheme to enhance the separate elements of the elevations. All colours are muted and have helped considerably to assimilate the variations between old, repaired and reconstructed brickwork.

The general attitude adopted throughout this project has been to repair the buildings to their appearance as they were when last occupied as family houses some 20 years ago. Cheap and makeshift repairs have been stripped away while late 18th and early 19th century modifications have been left and in some cases reinstated to allow the visitor to identify, through these features, the story of the buildings. In the same spirit new partitions have been inserted in a simple and functional way with no attempt made to conceal or deceive the observer about the date of construction.

The renovated properties were sold freehold, the special interest of the trust in the historic fabric and detailing being safeguarded by covenant. Despite the extreme circumstances, the balance sheet showed a small 'profit' — in reality, since the trust is a charity, a contribution to its rolling fund.

The major contributor to the financing of the scheme was the HBC. At the time of the Spitalfields scheme greater attention was being paid by the HBC to the need in some cases to extend grant aid to emergency works, and it was therefore able to consider favourably applications by the trust for both emergency aid (100 per cent) and also aid towards the main contract.

Again of crucial value was a loan, secured on the properties, from the AHF. Other financial contributions were received from the Seven Pillars of Wisdom Trust and the Idlewild Trust, together with several commercial organisations, including an invaluable interest-free loan from the Frizzell insurance group, which had a particular interest in the scheme as their own headquarters offices face 5 and 7 across the street.

In this way, two empty derelict properties, previously in mixed use and in a poor city district, were completely repaired and modernised as family houses. In terms of the wider area, 5 and 7 Elder Street have become symbols of the much-needed regeneration of the older parts of Spitalfields. Since the sit-in by trust members, no further listed building demolitions have taken place, despite the continued existence of closing orders and dangerous structures notices. The repair of other Georgian houses has been carried out nearby in Folgate, Fournier and Princelet streets, all schemes following the initiative or assistance of the Spitalfields Trust. No 27 Fournier Street was acquired with the help of a loan from the Baring Foundation.[1] In its belief that established businesses should be encouraged to stay in Spitalfields but that eighteenth-century houses are best used for living in rather than for non-residential uses, including in one case a room at 18 Princelet Street used as a beansprout farm, the trust has converted a derelict factory building in the area to workshops. This is now being used by garment-manufacturing firms, formerly occupying some of the finest early eighteenth-century rooms in London.

Considerable public interest was shown in the Elder Street scheme, and local councillors, residents and residents' groups followed the course of the work at every stage. The reintroduction of residential accommodation in the area is seen as a contribution towards arresting the decay and decline in that part of the city. Since the drama of Elder Street began to unfold in 1977, the residential population of the immediate area has increased from no more than half a dozen to several hundred.

The scheme has many admirable aspects, but the outstanding feature was undoubtedly the initial, decisive occupation of the properties by members of the trust, remaining there twenty-four hours a day by rota and without lighting, heating, water or sanitation, until the threat of demolition had been removed, a daunting performance that was later repeated to save an Arts and Crafts school in Spital Square. This determined action was itself founded upon a careful market assessment of the houses, their location and quality. The risk had been calculated. Even the solution to the water storage needs of the houses was characteristic of the trust's robust and imaginative style. In order to conform with the water authority's by-laws, it was necessary to install a non-standard long, low tank in the shallow roof spaces. With the economic constraints on the works, a specially made tank was out of the question but eventually a solution was found in the shape of a standard galvanised cattle trough.

3

THE COUNTRY HOUSE
AND ITS COMMUNITY

General

A report[1] commissioned by the British Tourist Authority and published in 1974 was pessimistic about the survival of country houses. At that time there seemed no reason why the sorry catalogue of decay and destruction — estimated to account for 270 major houses lost, reduced or derelict in England and Wales in post-war years, and many more including lesser houses — should not continue. Since then the outlook has improved. Although more houses have been lost, increasing numbers have been saved, given a new lease of life and, being no longer required for the role for which they were originally built, a new purpose.

At least part of the impetus for this turn around dates from an exhibition, also in 1974, at the Victoria and Albert Museum; 'The Destruction of the Country House' generated such interest that a permanent organisation, SAVE Britain's Heritage, was set up in the following year to give publicity to buildings threatened with demolition, before it was too late. SAVE is a charity, funded by bodies such as the Monument Trust, the American Express Foundation and the Yorkshire Tourist Board, and it has pursued its task courageously and effectively.

From the start, SAVE has always placed special emphasis on the possibilities of alternative use for historic buildings and, in a number of instances, has prepared its own schemes for reuse of threatened properties. SAVE has also published numerous reports on threatened buildings and organised exhibitions. The subject material has covered buildings of all types: Billingsgate Fish Market, Battersea Power Station, the Mansion House Square proposals, railway architecture and textile mills have all received close attention as, indeed, have country houses. In one of SAVE's publications,[2] a powerful case was made for retaining the residential use of country houses, respecting their basic structure and setting, and re-creating the residential community which they were originally constructed to house. An analysis of a number of plan forms showed each to be capable of subdivision, and problems at first sight appearing impossible and enormously expensive were shown to be capable of solution. The lesson from this and the example of a number of privately financed renovations and conversions indicate that the essential ingredient in solving the problem of derelict country houses is a degree of imagination on the part of the owners and their advisers, rather than a huge sum of money.

When Christopher Buxton of Period and Country Properties first became engaged in this field in 1954, the generally accepted view was that the only options available to hard-up owners of country houses were either to open them to the public or, if this was not practicable, to sell or convert them for institutional use. But not every house is important enough to open to the public and produce a useful income, and the risk of institutional use, particularly in the commercial sector, has been shown to be that the successful institution may outgrow the building and require additional accommodation in the grounds. This can threaten the integrity of the house and, equally important, its setting, very often one of its most valuable features. It can also destroy its homely qualities. Gradually the notion has developed, in the shape of a number of Period and Country Properties conversions, that the multi-occupation of country houses with their different areas and wings used by different groups of people, is nothing less than a tradition continued and brought up to date. Buxton suggests that one of the chief attractions of such schemes is that the residents have a few beautiful rooms in which to live but not so many that they become a headache to look after.

This theme was echoed and underlined in the SAVE report. It pointed to the variety of purchasers that had been and would continue to be attracted to life in a country house conversion: bachelors, retired couples, families with young children, weekenders, and people working in a town or abroad but requiring a base in the country. Many would like something unusual in character, hesitate to buy an isolated cottage or vicarage and seek the reassurance and company of neighbours living nearby. About his own flat in part of a Grade I listed house in Oxfordshire, Buxton commented, 'What I like about it is that when I drive up to it at night, it is not dark and deserted. There are lights and people around.'[3]

The SAVE report, its third on the subject, looked at some of the long-standing and apparently difficult cases of decay, chosen to illustrate both a range of layouts and plans and a geographical spread across the country. Kit Martin, formerly an architect and co-author with Marcus Binney of the report, drew up plans and approximate costings for the conversion of each plan type into a number of self-contained residences. It concluded that the cost of the rescue of these houses need not be significantly more than the cost of good quality new housing of equivalent area; that the basic price might well be covered by sale values; and that other than in exceptional circumstances grant aid, whether from public or private sources, was important for elaborate ornamental architectural features — not vital to the function of the house, but essential to its character — rather than for the basic elements. In effect, the report said that, given a little help, the country house could pay its way, and in its case studies it indicated, in planning terms, how.

SAVE identified two principal house types: in the first group — those with a shallow plan — there are a number of variants, comprising U, H, L or courtyard-shaped plans and the simple linear plan. Pursuing the Buxton theme of the residential community, each of these plans normally converts readily whilst retaining the principal elevations intact, preserving interiors of special character, respecting structural divisions, and forming, in effect, terraced houses with a difference. Bath, Brighton, Buxton, Leamington Spa and the Bloomsbury and Regent's Park areas of London benefited from the grand terraced house in the eighteenth and early nineteenth centuries. The concept of the country-house conversion is not dissimilar, though in a country rather than a town setting.

With the second principal type — a deep plan — a different approach is needed. These tend to be smaller houses, villas rather than mansions, constructed vertically around a staircase, or alternatively a courtyard house with the court filled in to form a central hall. With these it is more appropriate to adapt the house as flats, opening off the staircase or hall which become communal spaces. Some large houses are a combination of both types. In the last few years, these principles have been put into practice to rescue several important houses in a parlous, sometimes roofless state.

Barlaston Hall, Staffordshire

For some time, a large noticeboard stood prominently in front of the main entrance at disused Barlaston Hall, near Stone, reading 'KEEP OUT. This building is dangerous. The owner will not accept liability for any accident or damage, injury or death.' In the early 1980s, the style and message had changed to 'This building is being repaired and will be converted to flats by the Barlaston Hall Trust', signifying not only a change of attitude but a change of ownership in unusual circumstances. Barlaston Hall was bought by SAVE Britain's Heritage in October 1981 during the course of a public enquiry which was considering an application to demolish by the previous owners, the Wedgwood

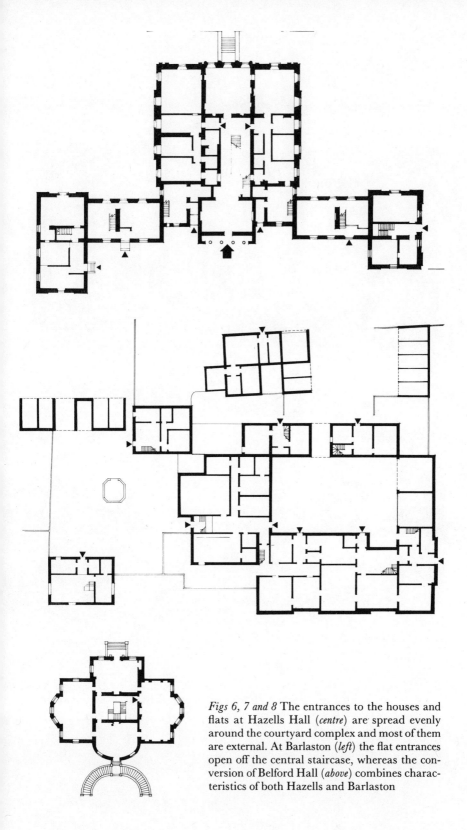

Figs 6, 7 and 8 The entrances to the houses and flats at Hazells Hall (*centre*) are spread evenly around the courtyard complex and most of them are external. At Barlaston (*left*) the flat entrances open off the central staircase, whereas the conversion of Belford Hall (*above*) combines characteristics of both Hazells and Barlaston

Fig 9 Even in its run-down state, mid-eighteenth-century Barlaston Hall was a proud building. It is a distinctively English development of the Palladian style imported from Italy by Inigo Jones over a century earlier

company. Towards the end of the enquiry, the company offered the Hall and 1¾ acres of land for sale for £1, on condition that restoration was carried out within five years. SAVE thereupon purchased the title.

The house, built in 1756 and attributed to Sir Robert Taylor (1714–88), architect of Heveningham Hall, the grandest Georgian mansion in Suffolk, had been acquired by Wedgwood in 1937 when it decided to move from its original works at Etruria to set up a new factory and model village at Barlaston, now a much sought-after residential area and winner in recent years of the prize as the best-kept village in Staffordshire on more than one occasion. The immediate setting and outlook from the house itself has changed little over the last century, but since the 1960s, despite its Grade I listing and despite offers of grants from the HBC, it had been empty and allowed to deteriorate to a dangerous state.

Barlaston is part villa, part mansion. It shows how the earlier Palladian villa style of Lord Burlington and William Kent was developed into a wholly English mode in the mid-eighteenth century. Built of brick over a rusticated base, there are four main floors, the principal storey containing the hall, saloon, library and dining-room being at first-floor level. It is a proud, erect building but by the time SAVE made its purchase the roof was leaking, floors and fireplaces had been removed and many internal finishes had deteriorated badly. Fortunately, a surprising amount of fine plasterwork and woodwork survived in the principal rooms.

In addition to the normal deficiencies of a dilapidated building, there was evidence at Barlaston of even more serious damage arising from the effects of coal-mining in the area and the likelihood of further subsidence as mining continued. At the 1981 public enquiry, SAVE's task was to demonstrate that, in spite of the extremely adverse circumstances, the renovation of the house was practicable as well as desirable. Its case was in two main parts: the cost, less possible grants, of the structural/conversion work, including the need to combat differential settlement, and the likely market value of the house when completed.

The attractive setting and outlook and the popularity of Barlaston village nearby suggested a residential scheme. The rooms of the house open off a central top-lit staircase, so it was decided to plan on the basis of flats leading off a communal space incorporating the staircase, main entrance and hall. The residents would approach from one side and look out on to the gardens on the other. The structural system proposed, providing new concrete ground- and basement-floor slabs and

Fig 10 Barlaston

new concrete walls at basement level, fitted in with these plans. But before the enquiry was over, SAVE had accepted Wedgwood's challenge and become the owner of the house itself.

SAVE's next move was to set up a charitable trust, the Barlaston Hall Trust, to carry out the restoration and conversion. The task of the new trust has been complicated by difficulties with the NCB over compensation for past damage attributable to mining activities. However, in order to make the building secure and watertight, repairs have been concentrated on the exterior and in particular on the roof. New lead was laid, all the roof slopes were reslated, for the first time in many years making the house dry and, with the aid of an RAF helicopter, two ball finials were retrieved from the grounds and reinstated high up on their plinths on the roof parapet. A substantial grant towards this work has been received from English Heritage and the project has also received generous funding from the National Heritage Memorial Fund and the Manifold Trust. The house is to be used as a museum until all matters are resolved with the NCB when the proposed conversion to four units will go ahead.

Belford Hall, Northumberland

On the map, Belford appears to be remote. It is roughly equidistant from Newcastle to the south and Edinburgh to the north and about 50 miles from both, but good road and rail links reduce the journey times. The town suffered from repeated border raids and was described in

86

1639 as 'the most miserable, beggarly town, or town of sods that ever was made in an afternoon of loam and sticks'.[4] Now, with a population of about one thousand, most of its buildings are relatively modern, but in 1756 its unappealing image did not deter Abraham Dixon, a London manufacturer and merchant, from commissioning James Paine to build a handsome Palladian house on the southern edge of the town. John Dobson of Newcastle added the wings in 1818. The estate, including a fine park, was acquired in 1923 for quarrying and in the 1930s the east wing was partially converted into flats. The house was requisitioned by the army during World War II, after which work on the house continued for a few years until halted due to lack of funds. When it was acquired by Northern Heritage Trust for £14,500 in 1984, vandalism had taken its toll; there was water coming through the roof and partial collapse at the rear.

Northern Heritage Trust was established in 1982, not as a competitor to the several existing conservation groups in the north of England, but to operate in areas they do not cover or where their resources are at full stretch. It was set up on the existing administrative base of the North East Civic Trust — its secretary, Neville Whittaker, is also director of the NECT, one of the Civic Trust's four regional associate trusts — and it covers the counties of Tyne & Wear, Durham, Cleveland and North Yorkshire as well as Northumberland. A similar trust was established at the same time in the North West. Northern Heritage has already become involved in a wide range of projects throughout the region, sometimes as an agency working for other organisations wishing to capitalise on the special conservation know-how it has to offer, sometimes on its own account on a revolving basis on similar lines to many other trusts, and sometimes, as at Belford Hall, with new and unpredictable ventures.

The trust became involved at Belford through the DoE and a study group on housing in villages set up by a northern consortium of housing authorities. At first, without detailed ideas as to what the hall could be used for and with only a limited budget, the intention was simply to renovate the main structure and to resell it in a sound but unconverted state, but notional schemes indicated that housing in one form or another was likely to be the best and most beneficial use. Amongst other uses, conversion into an hotel was looked at, but the effect on the integrity of the building was found to be disastrous.

However, with the financial support and advice of the Monument Historic Buildings Trust, work on the restoration and conversion into a number of quality houses and flats was started. Others that gave crucial support include SAVE, the Sir James Knott Trust, the Pilgrim Trust, English Heritage and the Countryside Commission. Once the work is completed and the properties are sold, the freehold interest will be transferred to a management company, Belford Hall Ltd, for it to grant 125 year leases to purchasers. All lessees automatically become members of the management company, which has responsibility for the provision of basic services, the upkeep of the grounds and common parts, and the maintenance of the structure. The lessees are responsible for internal repairs and upkeep, the cost of services and rates for their separate properties, together with a proportion of the service charge.

The prolific output of James Paine (1716–98) is well represented in the north of England, perhaps nowhere better than at Belford. The renovation is designed to respect the exterior and interior of the house and its setting. Communal areas, such as the entrance hall and conservatory, are furnished by the trust, and the original carriageways and drives have been reinstated. Where room heights have to be modified to suit modern living requirements, the old ceilings are repaired and retained above the level of the inserted ceiling. A window on the principal staircase has been entirely rebuilt in accordance with Paine's design. In the wings there are some discreet internal modifications, but externally they are restored to look as Dobson built them.

Whilst all the work is based on a carefully thought-out and detailed

Fig 11 The wings were added at Belford by Newcastle architect John Dobson in 1816. Paine's original design was for a pair of longer and lower symmetrical wings which repeated the pediment of the main block

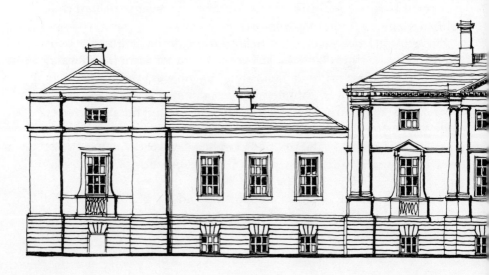

overall plan, the financing, as at Hazells (see below), depends on the sale of individual units paying for the next, and so on. Strict covenants, aimed at preserving the architectural quality of the house and its setting, are written into the leases. Letting is the responsibility of a local estate agency, but it is being handled on a national basis with the aid of a high-quality published account of the scheme. 1986 should see Belford's new residential community in being.

Hazells Hall, Bedfordshire

Hazells Hall near Sandy has an open courtyard plan, dating from the early and late eighteenth century. The house is for the most part one or two rooms deep, laid out around two courts. It is a dignified building, characteristic of its period, and located about 10 miles from Bedford and 4 from Biggleswade. An application to demolish was made in 1979 after several attempts to find an institutional tenant had failed, but following a public enquiry at which SAVE gave evidence, the application was refused. The house was purchased in 1981 by Kit Martin, who had ceased practising as an architect in 1976 to set up as a builder, for conversion into self-contained houses, flats and cottages. Included in the sale were 14 acres of garden.

At the time of Martin's purchase the house had a sorry appearance. For many years sections of the roof had been leaking, parts of the building had collapsed or were affected by dry rot, windows were broken, the grounds overgrown. But on the credit side the external elevations showed only minor structural faults, every part of the interior had a wealth of good detail and the courtyard form of the comparatively

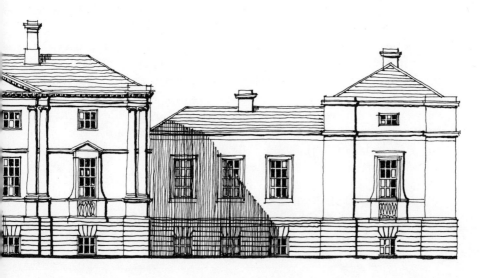

narrow plan was ideal raw material for conversion into a number of dwellings. Twelve houses and flats have been provided, having one, two, three and four bedrooms with entrances spread around the complex. A middle-sized unit has approximately 2,300 sq ft of floor area, twice the size of an average three-bedroomed house. Because of the quality and character of the house, the rooms are in some cases large, ideal for the purchaser who owns bulky items of furniture and is looking for easily managed accommodation with a few spacious rooms and an historic ambience.

Restoration work began early in 1982. It was tackled in stages, which had the advantage of not only reducing the initial capital outlay, but enabling small firms or individual craftsmen, who would be unlikely even to attempt an estimate for the whole job, to undertake the work or part of it. Otherwise, it would be left to the larger contractors with their higher overheads and, very likely, higher travelling costs. A preliminary estimate showed that, whereas the total cost would be almost £700,000, the restoration of a typical dwelling would amount to less than £60,000, an attractive size of job for most local builders. Continuity of work for the individual building trades can be achieved by negotiating rates for the next stage as soon as work is started on the first. Once established on the site, a builder will normally be keen to carry on with subsequent stages, but if for some reason negotiations on rates fail, it is still possible to invite tenders from others. In the event, Martin employed his own staff for most of the principal trades.

By early 1985 only the summer house awaited occupation, the remainder enjoying the fresh air of residential use for the first time since before World War II. The former owner, the Rt Hon Francis Pym, MP, now lives in a modern house in the park and is pleased with the outcome, but things must have looked differently in 1979 after a fruitless eleven-year search for an appropriate tenant. The turning point had come in 1968, when the lease taken by Bromham Hospital expired and the hospital, to the surprise of the owner, decided against renewal. The Pyms' new house was already under construction. Then followed the long search for a new tenant for a building that, even before the hospital left, was beginning to suffer from years of minimum maintenance, starting with the occupation by the Women's Land Army at the outbreak of the war. Particularly in the late 1960s and the early '70s, it is easy to believe that the building was not commercially attractive and that its architectural worth, even as the tide in favour of conservation was turning, was considered of only secondary importance when compared with other houses at risk at the time. Reluctantly, and as it turned out

Plate 20 With its powerful arched theme, Kirkaldy's in Southwark Street, London, combines the utilitarian virtue of strength and durability with that of decorative appeal *(Civic Trust)*

incorrectly, demolition was seen as a necessity, even though it would erase the architectural outcome of over two centuries of custodianship by the Pym family. Had it not been for the ingenuity and determination of the new owner, with his economical direct labour method of carrying out the work, Hazells could easily have gone the same way as many other lost country houses. But three years' restoration work turned what may have seemed to some a pipe-dream into the reality of a new and evidently marketable chapter in the history of the house.

Hazells Hall is one of several major houses to be restored and converted by Martin. In 1976 he had acquired Dingley Hall, near Market Harborough in Northamptonshire, an impressive complex of buildings of sixteenth-century origin that was given a pedimented extension and remodelling towards the end of the following century, attributed by Pevsner to Hugh May but now thought to be the work of William Winde. From 1958, when it appears to have been in good order, it suffered from a series of ownerships and vandalism, and when Martin became the owner it had become little more than a shell, the investment and careful husbandry of four hundred years all but tossed aside in fifteen. It then took three years to adapt and reconstruct the house into eleven houses and flats in five stages. Dingley is in the heart of the Midlands, within 20 miles of several major towns, and properties sold as soon as they became available, often before they were completed.

Although originally a courtyard plan like Hazells, Dingley is now a variant of the H-plan, but within the rambling complex of Gunton Hall, Norfolk, another Martin project, there are characteristics of several plan types pieced together in two spates of activity in the 1740s and the 1780s, first by Matthew Brettingham and then by James Wyatt. The contents were dispersed at a major country house sale in 1980. Parts of the buildings have been little altered since they were built, others are ruinous. The Martin scheme encompasses both fine rooms full of Georgian detail and modest service rooms and so naturally produces a range of accommodation, making it attractive to people of different ages and circumstances. Situated 22 miles from Norwich, 130 from London and with the North Sea close by to the north and east, Gunton is somewhat off the beaten track, in spite of which nearly all thirty units in the total complex, set in the large and spectacular park, lodges and gardeners' cottages included, have been completed and sold.

Plate 21 Two new properties were added on the corner site (left) after the renovation of Nos 5 and 7 Elder Street, Spitalfields (centre) had been completed *(Civic Trust)*

Fig 12 The church and the town hall are the two most important punctuation marks in Wirksworth's roofscape

4

REVIVING A WHOLE TOWN
WIRKSWORTH

Each town has its share of good and bad times. And what is good for some may be bad for others. For some people, the arrival of the railway in Wirksworth in 1867 may have been good news, but for the town as a whole it marked the beginning of over a hundred years of decline. The railway, linking with Derby and the national network, opened up immense possibilities for the quarrying and distribution of the limestone on which the town stands. A tunnel was even built below the town centre to connect the adjacent Dale Quarry with the railway sidings. The quarry flourished but it brought with it, to the very heart of the town, dust and noise on a scale that Wirksworth had never before experienced. All those who could afford to do so left, and most of the good buildings either became vacant, underused or were occupied by people with inadequate money to maintain them. Now, with its population of 6,900, it is hard to accept that Wirksworth was at one time the third largest town in Derbyshire.

Before the railway and the quarry came, Wirksworth had been a pleasant market, commercial and business centre. Even after a century of blight, the former prosperity of the town is still reflected in its buildings, the large cruciform church, dating from the thirteenth century, grand Georgian town houses, the nonconformist chapels and a fine vicarage built in 1831. As late as 1871, there was sufficient confidence to conceive and build an impressive Town Hall; 103 years later, local government reorganisation removed control of most of the town's services to the new West Derbyshire District Council — a further blow on top of all its other deprivations.

It was Wirksworth's record of a century of bad luck, evidenced in its run-down streets and buildings, together with their intrinsic attractive qualities and potential for improvement, that influenced its selection for a prototype regeneration project — for a change a piece of good luck. Sponsored initially by the Monument Trust, one of the charitable trusts of the Sainsbury family, the project was the brainchild of the Civic Trust and the objective no less than to reverse the decline of a hundred years. It was seen as a prototype in the sense that there seemed no reason why the practical results and lessons should not be applied in the many broadly similar situations elsewhere. The Civic Trust set itself five basic aims to be carried out, as far as it was possible to do so, over a three-year period. The aims[1] were to encourage:

1   Everyone to have a sense of pride in Wirksworth, as well as an increased awareness of its attractive qualities, all of which it was intended to cherish and enhance.
2   More people to live in and to take more care of the older properties in the centre.
3   The provision of more job opportunities to enable people to both live and work in Wirksworth.
4   Greater investment by residents as well as visitors in the town's shops and businesses.
5   The development of the town's tourist potential as part of a scheme to improve the economy.

To further these objectives, the Civic Trust sought as the top priority a foundation of firm public support with the people in the town itself. But before going public, a crucial meeting had been held at which appropriate members of the county, district and town councils had met the Civic Trust representatives and endorsed the aims of the project. The town council thereupon called for a public meeting to be held at the Town Hall in November 1978.

It soon became clear that the Civic Trust, as an independent non-political outside body, was in a good position to bring the various interests and parties together in the concerted effort that was so essential. But as an outsider, without the wealth of knowledge about Wirksworth and the surrounding area possessed by local people, the trust was intent on launching the project on a broad front, to adopt an encouraging rather than an imposing role and to stress that nothing would be achieved without the support of the people of the town. The public meeting was well attended, and after the trust had outlined the objectives, it quickly emerged that Wirksworth was going to give them its enthusiastic backing.

But the timing of the meeting, at the onset of winter, was not ideal. The town was keen to get the project started but in its first vital months, during which outdoor survey work was required, roads and surfaces were frequently covered in snow and at times poor visibility hampered progress. The climatic difficulties were compounded in the early months by the project's lack of a local base from which to work, for meetings, as a visible presence in the town or simply as somewhere in which to shelter. These handicaps made it difficult to produce quick results in response to the enthusiasm of the public meeting, which, with hindsight, should have been held in the spring or early summer.

The project team was led by the Civic Trust's consultant architect, Gordon Michell. Fortunately, an offer from a Derbyshire firm of architects of almost exactly the right accommodation to serve as the team's base came immediately after the public meeting. Centrally situated, it was formerly a coach house and stables which the firm, Sebire Allsopp, was planning to restore and convert into offices for its own use. There was sufficient space to allow for an office for the team and a shared room for meetings, both on the ground floor. It would have been ideal if it had been available for occupation straightaway, but the conversion work still had to be done and for the first few months the wintry conditions delayed progress. It was not until August 1979 that the project team finally moved into its headquarters.

However, the intervening months were used to explain the aims of the project to the many societies, clubs and organisations in the town — the civic society was the first of several to arrange a special meeting, usually in the evening, for this purpose. Among the long list of organisations visited by Michell were the sixth form of the Anthony Gell comprehensive school (the most senior of the town's four schools), the Wirksworth Ladies Group, the Chamber of Trade and Commerce and the Rotary Club, as well as the town, district and county councils. The message was simple: that the whole town needed to be involved if the project was to succeed. But there were some signs of impatience as the winter snow gave way to warmer days and the project team were acutely aware of the need to produce tangible results as quickly as possible.

To involve the town, it was essential for the wishes and opinions of the townspeople to be known and understood. The meetings had been helpful but did not give a true picture, representative of the community as a whole, so to obtain a fuller impression of those aspects of Wirksworth which local people considered important, good or bad, an independent research consultant, Alan Hedges, was commissioned to carry out a survey and produce a report. Using quota-sampling methods, six groups were assembled — each group comprised fifteen members — forming a cross-section of the people in the town. Between March and May 1980 each group had two meetings, at the first of which Hedges led the discussion with the project leader listening in. At the second, Michell gave the team's response and this was in turn responded to by the group. Also, with the help of civic society members and others, leaflets inviting written comments were distributed to every household, and a discussion was held with sixth-formers at the comprehensive school.

In this way, Hedges created a picture of what the people of Wirksworth thought of their town and wanted for it. Roughly in order of importance and in very brief summary, the following appeared to be their opinions and wishes:

1 The town centre: it was strongly criticised as being drab and dirty.
2 Character: the basic qualities of the town, its old buildings, narrow winding streets, stone setts and other traditional features, were liked.
3 Old buildings: there was reluctance to see buildings demolished but uncertainty concerning the feasibility of repairs and a suspicion that expensive restoration might increase values and put them beyond the pockets of local people.
4 Neglect: comment was made about the number of empty properties and the lack of maintenance of even the houses, shops and other buildings that were in use.
5 Obstacles to improvement: the attitudes of certain property owners, a distrust of change, resentment at interference by outsiders, lack of knowledge about grant availability, and doubts as to the suitability of local builders for repair work were all seen as difficulties.
6 Excessive litter and dirt: blame was attributed to a badly sited rubbish skip, from which rubbish was blown back into the town, school-children, chip shops, the market and the deterioration in standards since West Derbyshire District Council took over the street cleaning and refuse collection functions from the former urban district.
7 Lack of amenities: there were few entertainment facilities for teenagers, the south end of the town needed a children's playground and the elderly needed a day centre. It was also difficult to find out about facilities that were available. There was a feeling that those at the comprehensive school should be more fully used by the community.
8 More local jobs: although unemployment was not particularly high, many people who commuted did so reluctantly and it was considered that there was a need for more local jobs for those who wished to work in the town.
9 Traffic: lorries especially and through traffic, posed a danger to pedestrians in a town of narrow streets and pavements; it disturbed people's lives, kept them awake at night, caused vibration which damaged buildings, spread dirt and splashed it on the walls and windows of shops and houses. There was strong opposition to the increase in lorry weights that was being considered by the government at the time.
10 Parking: it was considered that off-street car-parking provision was inadequate, while on-street parking caused congestion and danger. However, while off-street parking remained inadequate, it was unreasonable to limit severely the amount of parking in the street. Parking charges were considered to be damaging to traders.

11 Public transport: in spite of its importance to a town which looks to neighbouring places for jobs, recreation and all manner of services, public transport was thought to be expensive and provide a poor service. High fares and poor services discouraged use, existing services were considered unreliable and they ran only north-south.

12 Public lavatories: the poor state of the public lavatories caused offence and worry.

13 Quarry dust: the dust blocked drains and made buildings dirty, even inside. The problem was believed to have worsened over the years and there was support for tougher enforcement of working practices.

14 Shops: there were two contrasting, yet linked, viewpoints. It was said that Wirksworth should support its local shops but they were criticised as uncompetitive, too expensive, offering too limited a choice, not being open when needed, not showing sufficiently attractive displays and having an uncaring attitude.

15 Community information: because of the difficulty in obtaining information of many different kinds, the project team's idea of an extended library providing an information service was supported.

16 General: there was a widespread conviction that council services had deteriorated since 1974, when Wirksworth Urban District Council ceased to run them and that the successor district council should look into ways of localising services and sources of information. There were complaints about poor street lighting and criticism of uneven roads and pavements, along with a wish to retain the traditional setts, to have the local police back on the beat and for improvements to the churchyard.

The project team found the survey both useful and encouraging in that in many ways it confirmed its own opinions and hopes. Discussions with the six groups both encouraged views and gave Michell the opportunity to respond. This pattern was clearly influential in shaping the result. But the team found that there was little understanding of the roles of the Civic Trust and the project, and that many living within a GIA designated by the district council knew nothing, surprisingly, of the council's proposals. Copies of the Hedges Report were deposited in the libraries at Wirksworth, Matlock and Buxton and distributed to town, district and county councils, the comprehensive school and the civic society.

LANDSCAPE APPRAISAL

Another consultant, Mary Mitchell, a landscape architect, was commissioned to look at Wirksworth in its setting and the visual qualities of the town itself, so as to provide a framework against which to assess any proposals for change affecting the appearance of the town or its immediate landscape. On the basis of a thorough survey, including footpaths and internal spaces within the town, Mitchell built up a catalogue of the best features of Wirksworth's landscape, and high-lighted those areas in need of improvement. Her report consisted of two large maps, a survey base and an overlay with her main proposals.

Taking account of these, the Civic Trust team produced a six-page leaflet with recommendations. It emphasised the rich opportunities for improvements but pointed out that they must be in tune with the robust character of the town: 'Wirksworth is a sturdy place and it must not be made to look like somewhere else — least of all prettified.' Recommen-dations were made under broad headings: the conservation area (desig-nated in 1970), the town's approaches, parking, walking, trees, local authority depots, housing, street furniture, the market place and longer-term issues. A table suggested who should be responsible for implementation and a concluding paragraph returned to the theme that little would result without a joint effort: 'Some of the proposals, such as tree planting, can be carried out by private individuals and voluntary organisations. Others could be undertaken with the help of one or other of the Manpower Services Commission programmes . . . Much depends on the local authorities. But they will not feel encour-aged to play their full part unless they have the support of the towns-people . . .' Within a matter of months the implementation of the Mitchell proposals began.

THE CIVIC SOCIETY

One of the factors that had led to the choice of Wirksworth for the pro-ject was the existence of a civic society. In the run-up to the launch in 1978, the support and advice of Councillor Bernard Truman, at that time both town mayor and chairman of the Wirksworth Civic Society, was of vital importance, but with the project under way the member-ship generally became involved. They gave invaluable help in many ways. Attractive postcards of the town were produced for sale at a profit at the society's meetings and in the shops. With the county planning department, the society produced, at 50p a copy, a wall sheet of over sixty drawings of the town. By March 1982 over one thousand copies had been sold, and the wall sheet has since been reprinted in a reduced format. In the summer of 1981 there followed a pocket-sized Town Trail, containing a short history of the town, plans, sketches and two town walks. Later the society marketed sets of notelets of the town based on drawings by a local artist. Each product appealed to residents and visitors alike and assisted the project in its aim of focussing atten-tion on the individual qualities of the town.

The civic society's assistance was given with the packaging and,

helped by comprehensive school pupils, distribution of project literature and also with a series of practical projects. A town monument was
cleaned, the church's early Georgian lych-gates and the market place
bus shelter were repaired, many trees and shrubs, together with long
lengths of hedgerow, were planted, tarmac was cleaned from limestone
setts and a number of overgrown footpaths leading from the town to the
countryside were cleared and reinstated.

During the course of the project, the membership of the civic society
doubled.

THE HERITAGE IN EDUCATION

Gordon Michell and his team placed high priority on the involvement
of the local schools. The Anthony Gell School sixth-formers had been
present at some of the early talks, and the headmaster came on a
number of occasions with parties of twenty-five pupils to the project
office to discuss problems and opportunities. A group carried out a
survey of clubs and societies and were surprised to discover a whole
range going quietly about their business, and published the results in
the form of a Town Guide. But, useful though this *ad hoc* activity was,
there was a need for a permanent structure to encourage and awaken
the interest of the young, and their parents, in their environment and
heritage. So in the autumn of 1979 a Wirksworth Heritage Education
Group was formed, sponsored by Derbyshire County Council as the
local education authority, on the basis of the Civic Trust's own Heritage
Education Group.[2] The Wirksworth group included the head and
senior staff of the four schools, local architects, planners, environmental
health officers and civic society representatives, and its aim was to
stimulate an appreciation of the local community and an understanding of Wirksworth, past and present. Although all four schools had
included environmental work in their curricula over the years, the
WHEG, arising out of the project, gave it new vigour and the extra
dimension of community involvement.

The four schools welcomed the help of many outside visitors, groups
from the two infant schools studied the market, the bakery, fire station,
mills and the old lead mines, and one class established a garden. Comprehensive school pupils carried out a land-use survey, sketched buildings and surveyed local industry. As all the work was rooted in the town
they knew, it gave history and geography a fresh reality. But the range
of activities stretched school budgets. Pump-priming financial help was
given to the three primary schools by the project and the education
authority; the Anthony Gell School was assisted by a grant from the

Morell Charitable Trust, while the project, community groups and local businesses supported the Town Guide and the WHEG received a donation from the local branch of the RIBA.

The schoolwork culminated in an exhibition, 'Our Town, Our Schools', in the parish church during the Wirksworth Festival week in October 1980. It was opened by Patrick Nuttgens, attracted a steady flow of visitors and made a favourable impact on attitudes and morale. More lasting results of the heritage education work were a local studies centre for second-year pupils at the Anthony Gell School and the use of outsiders with specialist knowledge to supplement and help the school staff — the town, and perhaps other places, should reap the benefits of these developments in the future.

THE COMMUNITY SCHOOL

High among the comments made at the Hedges meetings was the possibility of making better use, by the community as a whole, of the facilities at the Anthony Gell School. To follow up this idea the Wirksworth Community Education Council, the body required by the County Education Committee to monitor the local provision of youth and adult education, formed a working party, with project representation. It concluded in favour. The Education Council, the town council and a public meeting held in June 1981 gave the idea further backing. It was noted that the manifesto of the county council controlling group included a pledge in favour of the community use of educational resources, and in January 1982 the County Director of Education was formally requested to designate the Anthony Gell School a community school. Notwithstanding their sympathy for the idea, the constraints under which local authorities operate have so far prevented the county council from being able to do so.

THE TOWN HALL GARDEN

From the beginning, the project was supported by the town council, and after the original public meeting the council had voted £2,000 towards a project to be suggested by the project team. At the back of the Town Hall, with public access from the churchyard, was a run-down garden, largely forgotten and used mainly, it appears, for the clandestine feeding of stray cats which, not surprisingly, multiplied in number. But it was a sunny spot in the heart of the town with good views and seats could be provided. If improved, the town council, it was thought, would be seen to be setting a good example. The townspeople had other ideas. When the scheme was announced, Michell was assailed by numbers of people, not all of whom can have been cat lovers, who thought the scheme too expensive, an extravagance and a bad use of scarce resources. After all that had been said about public involvement, it was clearly impossible to proceed, and the team could do no more than wait for the controversy to subside. It was an unpleasant, disturbing but revealing episode, and in a short time added considerably to the team's knowledge about Wirksworth people and their priorities. The town council, too, were taken aback but fortunately continued to provide funds for the project from its annual budget.

A scheme with more support was soon developed. The team saw a chance to provide for two of the needs identified by Hedges — better public lavatories and, in an improved public library, an information centre. With funds provided by the district council, which recognised the poor state of the existing lavatories, it was proposed to relocate the public lavatories on a site close by. This released space to allow the library to expand from its cramped, windowless quarters, and within the extension to provide a section for community information. With the general goodwill and momentum built up by the project, the library scheme survived local authority budget cuts in 1979–80, and county, district and town councils agreed to contribute to the cost of building work. The cost of equipment was met by the Marsden Charitable Trust,[3] whose trustees have connections with Derbyshire, and work was able to start in autumn 1981, a gestation time of three years from the launch of the initial project.

OFFICIAL MEASURES FOR THE IMPROVEMENT OF THE TOWN

Even before the launch in 1978, the local authorities had accepted the need to help Wirksworth. This was influential in the decision of the Civic Trust when selecting the town as the subject for the project. The central area was designated a conservation area in 1970, becoming eligible for grants under section 10 of the 1972 Planning Act and, in August 1978, a few months before the public meeting, a GIA was declared covering 10½ acres (4.3 hectares) of housing west and north from the Market Place.

Many key buildings in the conservation area were in need of repair and qualified for grant aid, but this was unlikely to exceed 25 per cent of the cost and their owners were often unable to find the balance. Neither the county nor district councils was in a position to give the substantial help required. To reduce the proportion of repairs costs falling on the owners to 50 per cent, a Town Scheme[4] was established and publicised. In the first year (1979–80), the county and the district each contributed £3,000, matched by the DoE (HBC) to produce a total grants pool of £12,000. This was raised in each subsequent year. On this basis the annual repair work increased to a value, including owners' contributions, of £37,120 in 1982–3.

As well as generously helping with the Town Scheme, the HBC also made a block allocation to Wirksworth of £30,000 per year for three years to assist with conservation area grants. In this case the percentage level varied, but probably averaged 33 per cent.

CONSERVATION AREA EXTENSION

In her landscape report, Mary Mitchell had suggested a major extension of the conservation area to protect the setting of the town and include, on the east, the fields rising to the crest of the hills. The extension was agreed by the district council in 1979. It increased the number of buildings eligible for Town Scheme and section 10 assistance. In the first three years, fifty-one grants were made and in each year all the funds available were allocated.

GENERAL IMPROVEMENT AREA

It had been noted from the Hedges research in 1980 that some of those living within the GIA were unaware of its potential benefits or even its existence. The area contained 172 residential properties of which a number were empty and ruinous and thirty-one lacked inside WCs, fixed baths and hot water supplies, but even with the efforts of the district council GIA and project teams combined, the number of grants for housing improvements, especially favourable in a GIA, totalled only ten by April 1982. During a period in which improvement grants could account for as much as 90 per cent of the cost of the work, this was a disappointing figure for three years' GIA status.

In other respects, the amount of improvement work in the area was encouraging. A number of owners carried out work without grant, and a series of individually small but collectively important public works were funded via the GIA. These included the provision of a children's play area, parking space and handrails on steep footpaths and steps, the reinstatement of traditional stone setts, the removal of ugly concrete lamp standards and their replacement by wall-brackets, the realignment of a footpath for safety reasons and repairs in the traditional manner of the characteristic stone boundary walls to lanes and footpaths. The district council also established a local bank of salvaged materials for reuse in the course of the GIA programme.

The council regard the setting up of the project as of great help to its aims. The project, and particularly its team leader, became a useful communications link, co-ordinating the objectives of the GIA with those for the town as a whole and helping to establish a general climate of confidence.

Other measures to increase the money available for repairs and improvements to residential properties in the GIA and the conservation area were a scheme of special mortgage assistance by the Abbey National Building Society[5] and an offer by the project to pay for two years a percentage of bank loan interest charges in cases where, having taken advantage of all other assistance, a loan was still necessary. These various financial arrangements took time to arrange and, just as important, to publicise, but in spring 1980 the scaffolding began to appear. Once work started it began to spread, not only grant-aided schemes but some privately funded by owners wishing to avoid what they saw as the red-tape of grant procedures, and some by commercial owners who were ineligible for grant.

KEY BUILDINGS

Against the general background of its many humble, vernacular buildings, Wirksworth, like most other places, has a smaller number of key buildings, important on account of location, architectural or historic interest or townscape value. Without these buildings, any town is like a book without punctuation marks and the team was aware that in Wirksworth a number were at risk. In July 1980 it drew up a schedule totalling sixteen properties, in three categories of priority, which was discussed with a specially formed working party of the Derbyshire Historic Buildings Trust. The schedule was the basis of a revolving-fund operation supported by the Monument Trust and administered by the Historic Buildings Trust, which thereby became a valued partner in the project. It acquired and refurbished 1 The Dale as a shop and maisonette, the old blacksmith's shop at Dale End as a showroom, 31 and 33 The Dale as a single house, and 1, 2 and 3 Green Hill as offices, all of value to the street scene just off the Market Place and previously at risk. Nos 31 and 33 The Dale provided a test for the revolving-fund system. They were blighted by quarrying, deteriorating quickly, empty and had few architectural pretensions, yet with gap sites adjoining there would be a loss of all townscape continuity on that side of The Dale if they were not saved. But even allowing for grants, the Historic Buildings Trust calculated that renovation would result in a deficit of about £7,000. Because of the importance of the properties, the project and the trust agreed to share the risks and the pair of cottages were

renovated and converted as a single three-bedroom house.[6] The work was completed in the summer of 1980, formally opened by the chairman of the district council in September and sold soon afterwards as a family house. The final deficit at £1,800, of which the project paid 50 per cent, was less than had been feared.

JOBS

In the three years of the project, over £350,000 worth of work, directly related to grant aid, was carried out by local builders. For a place the size of Wirksworth, this was a considerable expenditure. This alone supported probably half a dozen jobs, a small but useful contribution towards the retention and creation of work in the building trade, especially in the traditional skills associated with repairs.

The Development Commission also desired to create jobs in the town and it agreed to fund, jointly with the county council, the renovation at Green Hill by the Derbyshire Historic Buildings Trust for the purpose of creating jobs for white-collar workers who otherwise had to commute. Dating from 1631 and formerly one of Wirksworth's grand houses, 1, 2 and 3 Green Hill was little more than a ruin in 1978 and serious consideration was given to its preservation as such. But the trust had been involved, also with the Commission and the council, in a successful office refurbishment of a similar type in Ashbourne, and preliminary costings suggested that the potentially dramatic restoration of the Green Hill property could pay its way. To the surprise of some in the town, repair and reconstruction work started in the autumn of 1981.[7] It was completed by the end of 1983. The Development Commission, through the Council for Small Industries in Rural Areas (COSIRA), was also involved in an advance factory scheme of five units at Millers Green on the outskirts of the town.

None of this represents startling progress in job creation in the project's three years, but at least signs of new activity were to be seen, the exodus from the town was being halted and a few more people were coming into the town to work.

Fig 13 (top and centre) Although the renovation of 31–33 The Dale made a small loss, shared equally by the Wirksworth project and the Derbyshire Historic Buildings Trust, it is important to the town's conservation area and it now makes an attractive three-bedroomed house

Fig 14 (below) One of the options studied for 1, 2 and 3 Green Hill was to retain the building as a ruin, but with the help of the county council and the Development Commission it has been rehabilitated as offices by the Derbyshire Historic Buildings Trust

LOCAL SHOPS

As buildings in the town centre began to look more cared for, the prospects for shopkeepers improved. At the Hedges meetings the shopkeepers had been criticised for providing a poor service and the shoppers for failing to support the local shops, but there were some issues — the intrusion of heavy traffic in the town centre and the chilling effect on the Market Place of the removal of buildings on its north side in the 1960s for the construction of a new road, thereby funnelling traffic through the town even faster — for which neither shopkeeper nor shopper could blame the other or do anything about, certainly in the short term. In spite of the adverse factors, most shopkeepers did something in the course of the project to improve their premises, although shop window displays, interiors and opening hours, all criticised at the Hedges discussions, remained much the same as before.

Improvements and greater optimism attracted new shops — and jobs. Between 1979 and 1981, a bookshop, toyshop, pet shop, restaurant, delicatessen, lingerie shop, art gallery and coffee shop providing light lunches were opened. The two other branches of the lingerie shop were in Knightsbridge, London and Munich, rather than small market towns, but Wirksworth had been the factory base of the firm, Janet Reger, for over ten years. The Reger shop was clearly aimed mainly at markets beyond the town and all the new shops, in different degrees, looked to visitors as well as local people for trade.

TOURISM

From the outset it had been realised that Wirksworth was a town with a long history, much character and some fascinating buildings, equal in many respects to other places which were more favoured stopping places on the tourist map. Its history was one of Wirksworth's most important assets but so far it had been undersold. Yet each year visitors flock to the general area, the Peak District and the Derwent Valley. If some of these could be attracted to Wirksworth it would inject money and jobs into the town's economy.

In addition to the general improvements to the town's buildings and its shopping facilities, the team believed that further attractions, rooted in the unique qualities of the town, were needed. Two such schemes were developed. The first was for a heritage centre, to set out in an

Plate 22 James Paine's pedimented centre block at Belford Hall. Although it is contemporary with Barlaston Hall, Belford is a much more strict interpretation of the Palladian idiom *(Northern Heritage Trust)*

interesting and lively presentation the story of the town and how it now worked. The civic society took up the idea and invited the Civic Trust's Interpretation Officer, Arthur Percival, to talk on the subject. Following this, the society established a Heritage Centre committee to examine what could be done in Wirksworth. Finally, an independent study was commissioned in the spring of 1981 from the Centre for Environmental Interpretation at Manchester Polytechnic. The cost of the study was met with contributions from the Abbey National Building Society, the Carnegie United Kingdom Trust, the ETB, the National Westminster Bank, the town and district councils, the local chamber of trade and two of the larger businesses in the town. The study identified the main threads of the story, suggested who was likely to be interested, and outlined the facilities that would be required. The publication of the study was followed by the enthusiastic civic society's purchase of a near-derelict stone-built silk and velvet mill, only a few steps from the Market Place in which the society is establishing the town's heritage centre.

The other scheme was even more ambitious. It concerned the main industry of the town, stone quarrying, and the possibility of a centre, complementing that for the heritage, telling the story of this work. At first it was visualised in local terms, but the team soon found that others had already been thinking along similar lines, though more broadly based. Reports in 1979 by the Dartington Amenity Research Trust and in 1980 by the DoE with what was shortly to become the Stone Federation, were only the most recent manifestations of general interest in the stone industry and the need for self-promotion based on its history, its present and its future. The Dartington report had even suggested that a stone centre for this purpose should be established in Wirksworth. All of this brought about the formation of a Stone Centre Study Group, chaired by the project team leader, with the task of producing a prospectus and gaining wider support and financial backing.

Its location has always made Wirksworth a good base for holidays. By looking after its buildings, improving its shops and exploiting its history, the town should be powerfully attractive in its own right.

Plates 23 and 24 Except for its new, cared-for appearance, outwardly little was changed by the renovation of Hazells Hall even though it was adapted with its outbuildings to the needs of twelve families instead of the one for which it was originally built (*John Donat Photography*)

THE WITHDRAWAL OF THE CIVIC TRUST

The Civic Trust planned to withdraw from the project in April 1982, not because the work was finished, but because the essence of the project was to see what, if anything, could be done to improve a run-down town over a limited period and from this to attempt to draw conclusions which might be applicable in other places. In July 1981 the town council called a second public meeting, two years and eight months after the first, for the trust to report and to discuss the future. Although there was agreement at the meeting that the project should continue after the Civic Trust's deadline, there was no clear view as to how this might be achieved.

During the following months a plan, centred on a key role for Wirksworth Town Council, was worked out and agreed between the main parties. The town council, with the support of county and district officers, assumed responsibility for overseeing a further three-year period of work and established a steering committee made up of the mayor, three councillors and members of the two other local authorities. There would also be a working group of people committed to the project and in positions of influence, to include the county and district chief executives and planning officers, the county treasurer, representatives of the Derbyshire Historic Buildings Trust, the Conservation Area Advisory Committee, the Civic Society, the Wirksworth schools, the Chamber of Trade, the Rotary Club and the Civic Trust. The project leader, Gordon Michell, was retained as a consultant on a two days per month basis.

In the course of the project, the team and its leader had formed a good understanding with Barry Joyce, the county council's conservation officer and a Wirksworth resident, and its continuity was assured when he was seconded to take over Michell's role, spending half his time in Wirksworth with an office and telephone provided by the town council. The county council undertook to provide secretarial and accountancy services. To facilitate the raising of funds, it was recognised that the steering committee might eventually become an independent trust.

A full range of tasks and responsibilities — local, district and county — were identified by the departing Civic Trust to maintain momentum and keep the steering committee busy over the next three years. The Civic Trust withdrawal was formalised in April 1982, when Michell opened the extension to the public library, and the first meeting of the new steering committee followed in September. The future of the project was, appropriately enough, in local hands. The steering committee meets at intervals of about six months but Joyce keeps in weekly contact with its chairman. The committee soon began to make significant contributions to the direction of the second stage project, most notably in the areas of communications and community involvement.

From its earliest days, the original project team had sensed the crucial value of communications, particularly with the townspeople. It started producing a monthly newsletter, but after the first four issues other pressures diverted its efforts and thereafter it appeared, to the team's regret, only intermittently. The steering committee was concerned that the project's work was not widely understood and decided to seek the help of the *Matlock Mercury*, the local newspaper. The editor offered a half-page space per month and this has been a successful means of communication. In addition, a bi-monthly newspaper exclusively for Wirksworth was produced, financed through advertising, to widen further the scope for community involvement. It is edited by a member of the Anthony Gell School staff.

To encourage youth involvement, a project youth group was set up with an initial nucleus of sixteen pupils from the comprehensive school, charged with identifying and implementing its own specific objectives. In April 1984 it began to draw up a programme of activities. Two members of the group in rotation attend meetings of the steering committee with full voting rights.

These steps by the steering committee to improve public understanding and involvement were fully in line with the Civic Trust's objective of a firm base of public support from which to pursue its five original aims: fostering civic pride, better use and repair of older properties, more jobs, better investment in local shops and the development of tourism. It is appropriate to examine progress towards these aims during the first eighteen months of the second stage.

CIVIC PRIDE

The award of the prestigious Europa Nostra medal, announced in January 1983, for 'the exemplary regeneration of a small country town through a broad programme of self-help and innovative features which could be applied to other towns' must, by itself, have generated a fair amount of civic pride. Recognition on the European stage brought a spate of distinguished visitors to the town, talks about the project by Michell and Joyce in places as far afield as Brussels and Rome, and television and radio publicity.

Concern about litter at the Hedges discussions led to the town council forming, in June 1982, an Environmental Care Committee, to encourage better design, repair and maintenance in the streets. The committee has overseen a great improvement to all the town centre paved areas and launched a clean-up campaign featuring the town's Well-Dressing — an established annual event taking place over the spring bank holiday weekend — Queen and Ladies-in-Waiting wearing campaign T-shirts and accompanied by a small army of cubs equipped with refuse sacks. The schools, which contributed a poster exhibition by children on the clean-up theme, local voluntary groups and businesses, the local authorities and the statutory undertakers all participated in the objective of a cleaner and better looking town.

Improvements initiated by the new project leader are also under way for the village of Middleton-by-Wirksworth. These include the implementation by the district council of ideas produced by the children of Middleton School for the redesign of a vandalised playground and the implementation by the owners of a landscaping scheme for a prominent area of land in front of a public house at the entrance to the village.

Tree-planting aspects of Mary Mitchell's landscape proposals have been carried out by the county council in three locations. For the town council Joyce has prepared designs for new town signs, and a study is in hand for the redevelopment of the war memorial site, the last significant area of neglect in the town centre. Environmental education is now firmly established in the schools and wherever possible is taken to the point where ideas can be acted upon, as in Middleton. In the longer term, it is hoped to establish an Urban Studies Centre within the Heritage Centre to serve the whole of Derbyshire.

BETTER USE AND REPAIR OF OLDER PROPERTIES

Excluding Housing Act assistance, thirty grants were given in the eighteen months towards building repairs within the conservation area, leading to building work valued at more than £228,000. The work at 1, 2 and 3 Green Hill, 1 The Dale and the Blacksmith's Shop in Dale End has been completed, and the Derbyshire Historic Buildings Trust has been active in preparing and implementing a study for an area at the rear of the Market Place. The United Reformed Church has converted its former school rooms into a youth hostel and conference centre and the last of six renovated terraced houses in St Mary's Gate were occupied, the subject in 1979 of the first study commissioned by the project team. In 1983, the Abbey National Building Society, advised by the project leader, purchased a semi-derelict cottage in Green Hill with a view to carrying out an 'exemplary' modernisation.

114

MORE JOBS

The most encouraging development has been the attraction to the town, with the help of COSIRA, of a firm of children's clothing manufacturers. Between fifty and sixty jobs may be created. The town gained and the city lost when, in 1983, COSIRA and the Derbyshire Rural Community Council moved their headquarters to Wirksworth from Derby, and the attention of the chamber of trade and commerce has been drawn to the scope for an increase in tourist and leisure-related trade likely to arise from the development of the 725 acre Carsington Reservoir barely 2 miles from the town.

BETTER INVESTMENT IN LOCAL SHOPS

During the first eighteen months of the second stage, eight new retail premises were opened, mostly at the quality end of their trades, attracted by the historic flavour of Wirksworth. Some moved in from other towns and some were 'first-time' businesses. The chamber of trade was reminded that some of the Hedges criticisms had met with little response so far, but the chamber underlined the need for improved car-parking facilities. This has emerged as one of the main aspects now requiring the project's attention, perhaps in itself an indication of increased retail activity.

THE DEVELOPMENT OF TOURISM

The outline plans formulated in the first stage for the Heritage and National Stone centres have made impressive progress. By April 1984 the civic society had in hand or firmly promised £122,000 towards the Heritage Centre's projected £142,000 total capital cost, with major grants coming from the ETB, the DoE, the county and town councils and local industry. The society has formed a separate body, known as The Wirksworth Heritage Centre, to carry the plans forward to fruition.

Now backed by all aspects of the industry, the government, major grant-making bodies and the local authorities, the National Stone Centre has embarked on a life of its own, beyond Wirksworth and Derbyshire. The promotion committee has a membership drawn from the senior management of the participating bodies and plans have been drawn up and exhibited. In November 1983 the proposals were given a London launch at a meeting attended by the Parliamentary Under-Secretary of State for the DoE.

THE PROJECT REVIEWED

The Civic Trust was in the position of a respected umpire, but it had the additional power to influence the whole strategy of the match. From the first, it wisely took a modest line: 'we don't know all the answers', the inaugural public meeting was told, immediately convincing and establishing a bond with the people of the town. As quickly as it could, the trust secured a physical presence in the town and it had a tireless and knowledgeable project leader fully committed to his task. Some improvements would, in all probability, have flowed in any case from the local authority policies for the GIA, the recognition of the town's historic qualities in the designation of the original conservation area and the influence of a well-established civic society. The project built on these foundations, added its own fresh ideas, took time and trouble to involve the townspeople and gave improvement a new impetus and a broader base. Underneath, the Wirksworths of 1978 and today are the same, and if there were to be a new round of Hedges-type public discussions, it would doubtless soon be discovered that problems remain, yet the outward appearance of the town has been transformed, a start has been made on attracting new jobs and attitudes throughout the town are now more co-operative and positive.

Parallels to the various methods with which the transformation has been achieved may be seen, usually with less dramatic results, in countless towns. The difference in Wirksworth was that all the methods were used together in a short, sharp co-ordinated assault on the town's problems. The direct cost of setting up and staffing the project is estimated to be £25,000 a year at 1979 prices, about £4 per head of population, over a three-year period. For this comparatively small sum, the one-hundred-year decline of the market town was reversed. Many places on hard times must envy Wirksworth its change of fortunes. North of a line from Suffolk to Bristol, there can be few districts without its equally deserving case, but the outstanding and heartening lesson from the project is that the cost of the remedy need not be excessive. It should be well within the capacity of the authorities to raise locally, encouraged, perhaps, by a little central pump-priming, if all parties — official, voluntary and local people — are motivated to work together in the Wirksworth spirit.

5

CONCLUSIONS

With the sole exception of the National Trust for Scotland's trailer of events largely still to come, nothing comparable to the practical yet inventive conservation *oeuvre* of the 1970s and '80s existed in previous years, the time of the bulldozer rampant and comprehensive, and often highly speculative redevelopment. But it was the events of the 1950s and '60s that sowed the seeds of outrage and reaction, crossing party political, professional and social boundaries, that were to develop into a vigorous conservation lobby. As well-known landmarks disappeared or were engulfed by modern, oversized neighbours and places began to look more and more alike, so the streets and buildings that survived gradually became more highly prized, probably not so much for their architecture as for their reassuring sense of permanence. As Ronald Blythe expressed it in *The View in Winter*, 'The old absorb the familiar streets for as long as they possibly can. Where planners haven't muddled their ancient sequence the buildings and pavements become very special.'

Unease and even anger at development seemingly out of control, at first felt by a few, developed into a full-scale national organisation when, in 1957, the Civic Trust was founded to encourage 'the protection and improvement of the environment, particularly in towns, cities and villages', for the most part, in other words, in the built-up areas where the developers were at work. Across the whole complicated spectrum of environmental matters, touching on the very quality of life, the Civic Trust was able to articulate and give prominence to views that had previously been confined to individuals, more narrowly based organisations or town or county amenity societies. Within ten years, the trust had grown in influence to the extent that it was able to initiate and, in the form of a Private Member's Bill by its founder and president, now Lord Duncan Sandys, see new legislation through Parliament. The Civic Amenities Act introduced into the planning system the concept of conservation areas, and for the first time required local authorities to take account in their planning policies of the need to preserve whole streets and areas of towns as well as individual buildings. Aided by the

117

poor public image of unlet speculative offices, increasing doubts about the social consequences of high-rise living, alarm at the safety of certain building systems based on the new technology and the widespread public dislike of concrete, the new Act gave official sanction to the need for greater sensitivity in town planning. The change in emphasis immediately gave existing buildings a better chance of survival.

The chance has not been seized everywhere. Although the projects that have been described represent only a small part of an honourable roll-call of achievement, there are probably as many, or more that might have been, or could still be. It is not only in the depressed areas of high unemployment and low wages that empty, decaying buildings are a common experience. A 'barometer' small town like Rothwell in Northamptonshire — 1981 census preliminary count population 6,374 — neither of the north nor of the south, neither over-prosperous nor severely depressed, historic but industrialised by boot and shoe manufacturers and a worthy candidate for a Wirksworth-style programme of reinvigoration, has a ring of dilapidated, redundant, two- and three-storey brick and slate factories laying siege to the town centre conservation area. Within this are two of the county's most distinguished historic buildings: the parish church, very large, cruciform and partly Norman, and the Market House, a sixteenth-century gem, plus many Victorian and older buildings indicating Rothwell's importance throughout the centuries. The evidently persistent and buoyant demand for housing accommodation is met in the sprawling new estates, a massive capital investment consuming the hillside fields, ruinous to the town's setting and entirely dependent on private means of transport for access to work, shops and public facilities. From this investment the town centre benefits little — once the car is out of the garage more extensive shopping facilities than Rothwell's are within easy reach. Consequently, the town centre shops are not what they once were — some close on Saturday afternoons. A Kendal- or a Leiston-type conversion of the redundant factory buildings, by local authority, buildings preservation trust or private developer, or a combination of all three, could well provide attractive residential accommodation within a short walk of the library, the surgery and the shops, offer house purchasers a greater variety of choice than the estates alone provide and set in motion a move towards a more suitable setting and better days for the historic town centre and its ailing trade.

If the organisation of these projects has a common theme, it is that each is a response to local circumstances. The simple concept of making the best use of buildings that, superficially, appear unwanted and disfigure their surroundings has a broad enough appeal to attract support from various directions. Schoolteachers and businessmen, accountants and journalists, academics and lawyers, those whose profession is building and those from all political persuasions or none, all find common ground and a common enthusiasm, fostering pride and a spirit of self-help in people and places. The organisation required is adaptable to local requirements and situations. The enthusiasm is rooted in the community.

Surprisingly, it is not a field in which the community-based local authorities have been particularly active, even though the example of those that have shows that it can add a new and positive dimension to their work. The many routine tasks that councils perform rarely make the headlines, until something goes wrong. Typically, the well-oiled council machine operates without much fuss and, unfortunately, sometimes without a great deal of interest on the part of the community which it represents if the turnout in local elections is any yardstick. The imaginative renovation of run-down buildings is guaranteed to generate public interest and, particularly if it can be made to pay its way, admiration. In contrast, the do-nothing option is likely to lead to lack of maintenance of other buildings in the area, and vandalism and vermin may take over, all at a cost to the local police and public health services and the wider cost to the community as a whole in wasting assets.

Renovation, on the other hand, can have a snowball effect that puts the whole depressing sequence of spreading dereliction into reverse. As the spring 1981 newsletter of the Sussex Heritage Trust Society put it:

> It is gratifying to be able to report how much work has been done by other nearby building owners . . . to improve and repair their properties in this previously dejected corner of the town. If this is the result of the Trust's initiative — and we think it is — then it must give other building owners encouragement to start the ball rolling in other areas.

Seen from the town hall or the council offices, a revolving fund, run by the authority or in partnership with others, could avoid the hidden costs of building decay, remove long-standing eyesores, create permanent improvements that can be seen and used and become a part of everyday life, make a modest but useful contribution to jobs in the building industry, and perhaps even encourage greater public interest in and support for the authority's work as a whole.

In 1977 the DoE commissioned an investigation into the role of emergency repairs for run-down historic buildings.[1] The investigation

119

included a survey of the condition of listed buildings to which thirty-six local authorities throughout England responded, representing both historic and industrial towns, rural areas and the seaside. Although the principal and perhaps most significant finding was that few of the authorities had hard information, it was estimated that in their areas, about one-sixth of England (seven county and twenty-nine district councils), there were at that time about 4,000 listed buildings in bad or derelict condition yet still capable of being repaired. On a simple *pro rata* basis, this suggests something like 25,000 in the whole of England, or an average of about eighty in every local authority district. The data base is flimsy, but even half that number adds up to a massive obstacle to a civilised environment. It seems more likely that it may be an under-estimate. Since 1977, with the ongoing revisions to the old post-war lists, many more buildings have been added to the statutory lists of buildings of special architectural or historic interest so as to afford them the protection that was envisaged under the Act.

Buildings such as Rothwell's empty factories are unlikely ever to appear in the lists, having little architectural or historic interest in the accepted sense of those terms, but they constitute a resource of bricks and mortar, they express and depress the spirit of the places in which they stand just as much as a run-down listed building and, given the will and determination, are often capable of reuse for a new purpose. There are no figures, hard or soft, to quantify derelict unlisted buildings but they almost certainly outnumber their listed counterparts several times over. Everyday observation and experience should provide a sufficiently challenging statistic.

Because the projects tell the story of successful local initiatives, the role of central government is not emphasised even though it influences and sets the framework of regulations, finance and attitudes within which projects either flourish or wither. Different frameworks encourage or discourage local enterprise and effort, and produce more or less projects, more or less caring for places and communities. Since this takes place for the most part in the area of finely balanced profit and loss, the work is highly sensitive to any changes that affect the balance adversely. If the framework had been only slightly more favourable in recent years, there is no telling what might have been. But for the undiscovered Cinderellas there is no happy ending.

NOTES TO PART I

Bradford-on-Avon
(1) Architect Rodney D. Goodall.
(2) Based on *5, 6, 7 and 8 Market Street* by Elizabeth Stephenson. Published by the Bradford-on-Avon Preservation Trust 1982.

Essex
(1) See under Grant-making trusts.

National Trust for Scotland
(1) See under Grant-making trusts.
(2) Harling is a roughcast render in lime and small gravel applied to the wall so that the face of slightly projecting grit is left exposed.
(3) A forestair is an outside stair on the front of a building.
(4) The Regional Councils in Scotland are the equivalent of the County Councils in England.

Suffolk
(1) See under Selecting a builder.
(2) At that time the Civic Trust assisted the Department of the Environment with the administration of conservation area grant aid. It is now dealt with by English Heritage.
(3) Also known as ribbon or serpentine. They are characteristic of Norfolk and Suffolk, wavy on plan and thought to have been originally introduced from the Netherlands.
(4) In the manner of the buildings of Sir John Soane, architect, 1753–1837, acroteria are foliage carved or cast blocks on a parapet, often on the angles of a classical pediment.
(5) For the restoration of derelict land to a notional green field condition.
(6) See under Grant-making trusts.

Bristol
(1) Sir John Summerson. *The Shell Guide to England.*
(2) Architect Peter Ware.
(3) Architect Peter Ware.
(4) Architect Roy Moorcroft, Chief Architect, British Rail.

Derby
(1) Architects Sebire Allsopp with Derek Latham.

Edinburgh
(1) Marcus Binney and Max Hanna. *Preservation Pays. Tourism and the economic economic benefits of conserving historic buildings.* Published by SAVE Britain's Heritage.
(2) Other firms making donations were:
T. M. Gray & Associates

James Allen & Son Limited
Life Association of Scotland
John Menzies (Holdings) Limited
John Bartholomew & Son Limited
Jenners Limited
Cruden Developments Limited
A. Goldberg & Sons Limited
Scottish & Newcastle Breweries
RTZ Services Limited
Royal Bank of Scotland Limited
Clydesdale Bank Limited
Bank of Scotland Limited
Craig & Rose Limited
Lindsay's W.S.

London, Southwark
(1) A national organisation, the British Association of Friends of Museums, exists to support the work of local groups of Friends.
(2) See under Feasibility Studies.

London, Spitalfields
(1) See under Grant-making trusts.

The Country House and its Community
(1) *Country Houses in Britain — can they survive?* John Cornforth. Commissioned by the British Tourist Authority and published for them by *Country Life*.
(2) *The Country House: to be or not to be*. Published in 1982 with the aid of a grant from the Monument Trust.
(3) *The Country House in the 1980s*. John Young. George Allen and Unwin 1981.
(4) *The Shell Guide to England*. Michael Joseph Limited, Rainbird Reference Books Limited and Book Club Associates.

Wirksworth
(1) From *The Wirksworth Story: New Life for an old Town* published by the Wirksworth project in association with the Civic Trust in 1984 and available price £3.75 including p&p (1985 price) from the Corner Bookshop, 8 St John Street, Wirksworth, Derbyshire DE4 4DE. This gives a well illustrated account in full detail of the whole project.
(2) The Civic Trust administers the Heritage Education Group set up by the Department of the Environment in 1976. The Group brings together educationalists, planners, architects and others in order to stimulate environmental education at all levels, but particularly in schools. The Group's news sheet is distributed throughout the schools system twice a year.
(3) See under Grant-making trusts.
(4) See under English Heritage and local authority grants.

(5) In the late 1970s the Abbey National Building Society set aside part of its funds for special assistance to aid repairs in eighty areas of special housing need, of which Wirksworth was one. The scheme, operated in conjunction with the local authorities, was mainly intended to top up improvement and other grants and has since been followed by other building societies.
(6) Architects Sebire Allsopp, Wirksworth.
(7) Architects Derek Latham & Associates, Derby.

Conclusions
(1) 'Emergency Repairs for Historic Buildings' — a research project for the Department of the Environment by Michell and Partners, architects, 1a The Embankment, Putney, London SW15 1LB.

Part II — MEANS

6
ORGANISATIONS

The organisations behind the projects described in Part I were of five broad types:

1   Voluntary groups, based on a market town or a part of a large city.
2   Larger voluntary groups, based on a county area or a large city.
3   National voluntary groups.
4   County and district local authorities.
5   Joint local authority/voluntary alliances.

Each is capable of outstanding work and each can claim advantages not possessed by others. The smaller organisations can claim a close identity with needs at the grassroots and thereby a secure and useful future on a bedrock of local support. The larger ones have a better chance of ensuring continuity of work, making it easier to keep up the momentum and enthusiasm. Voluntary groups, small and large, usually have low overhead costs and recourse to grants and loans not available to official bodies, particularly if they are registered as charitable trusts. They are less directly affected than local authorities by public expenditure cuts and directives from central to local government and they are perhaps more likely to be able to rely on the sympathy and support of the public at large — useful when it comes to local fund raising. The local authorities have statutory powers and duties in the whole range of matters affecting run-down buildings, most notably in respect of buildings listed as being of architectural or historic interest, and they have a ready-made organisation with some, if not all, of the professional skills required. Local authorities are organisations of substance that may feel able to take on ambitious schemes which might deter the average trust or voluntary group. Most usefully they can reclaim VAT, and they are involved in any case in matters of environmental concern with or without their own positive renovation schemes.

But perhaps the greatest difference is that, whereas the local authorities have a multitude of functions, voluntary groups and trusts are set up for the specific purpose of practising conservation. This can give them a single-minded dedication to their task which it is difficult for the authorities to match. As has been seen, this sometimes works wonders, and it can amount to the full-time occupation of some of the key people involved. In other cases, it may be more difficult to find suitable people with the time and energy to spare; output then suffers. Significantly, out of seventy-five trusts registered with the Civic Trust up to 1984, the AHF has made loans to less than one-third.

Neither voluntary groups nor local authorities alone possess all the trump cards, but with an alliance the one can utilise the strengths of the other. Provided that they retain their independence, there is no reason why the two should not work together — the Charity Commission welcomes co-operation of this sort. Each party can benefit, as in the low-cost back-up the voluntary group can give to official policies and the statutory powers that can be held in reserve to support their joint objectives by the local authority.

For one reason or another, the alliance may not work everywhere, and if a different formula has already been successfully developed it is probably sensible to keep it unless circumstances change to make the established pattern difficult to sustain. The key people involved are generally in small groups, and changes in personnel may, for better or worse, have a crucial effect. Individuals are more significant than organisations: there can be no other explanation for the uneven and unpredictable distribution and progress of projects.

Plates 25 and 26 The charm of these redundant factory buildings in Rothwell, Northamptonshire, is well hidden but they are no worse than others that have been successfully given new life and purpose. It is important not to be deterred by first impressions

7

FORMING AND OPERATING A CHARITABLE TRUST

Most of the schemes described in Part I involved or were initiated and carried out by local historic buildings trusts. The number of these has increased significantly in recent years, prompted by Civic Trust reports to the then newly established Department of the Environment in 1971 and 1972 — 'Financing the Preservation of Old Buildings' and 'Forming a Buildings Preservation Trust' — followed by the coming into being in 1976 of the Architectural Heritage Fund for the purpose of providing the local trusts with low-interest working capital. The AHF first annual report in 1979 contained a register of thirty-eight trusts. The 1984 report contained seventy-five, including four that operate on a national basis; less than a quarter were solely registered charities, the majority also being companies limited by guarantee as well as being registered with the Charity Commission.

Trusts registering as a charity

The essential test of a charity is that its property must be applied to the benefit of the community and must not be the subject of claims or means by which profit is gained by private persons. In England, Wales and Northern Ireland it is the Charity Commission that advises a would-be charity if its objects make it eligible for registration; in Scotland the Inland Revenue carries out this function. Registration confers both privileges and obligations on the trustees. Exemption from income tax is absolute and rate relief is afforded by statute at the rate of 50 per cent, with local authorities having power to remit all or part of the rest. It is the Charity Commission's/Inland Revenue's task, once a trust is registered, to enforce the objects of the trust so that the trustees, present and future, are obliged to apply funds only to purposes that are strictly within the trust's defined aims. A registered trust must notify the

Plates 27–9 Often the full effect of the transformation to come may be difficult to visualise. Collin Croft, Kendal, before and after renovation *(Kendal Civic Society Building Preservation Trust)*

Charity Commission/Inland Revenue of any changes in the particulars which have been registered, such as changes in secretaryship or address of officers; it must maintain proper books of account, send a copy of the accounts annually to the Commission/Inland Revenue (in practice this is done quinquennially, but accounts may be called for at any time) and, if changed circumstances make this necessary, it must seek the consent of the Commission/Inland Revenue to any proposal to alter its objectives.

The following information is needed to enable an application for registration to be considered:

1   The title of the charity
2   A statement of its objectives
3   The proposed operational area
4   An indication of likely income
5   The name and address of the secretary and the address of any premises occupied by the charity
6   A copy of the latest accounts (if any)

At draft stage it is advisable to seek comment on the information to be provided before the application is finalised.

Registration enables a record to be assembled, nationally and locally, of all charitable bodies with objectives and resources which can be used for the public benefit. The effect of registration is to establish that the trust has an accredited claim to tax and rate relief.

Trusts registering as a company

Any seven or more persons or, if a private company, any two or more, by subscribing their names to a Memorandum of Association and by complying with the requirements of the Companies Act of 1948 in respect of registration, may form an incorporated company with or without liability. A buildings preservation trust which wishes to be a company will also normally be registered as a charity to obtain the benefits of both company and charitable status. A company returns its annual accounts to the Registrar of Companies, with a copy to the Charity Commission/Inland Revenue.

A company may be limited by guarantee without any share capital and, as a charitable trust, will not seek to make profits for distribution to its directors or to its shareholders. Members will not be entitled to receive any dividend, and any profits must be returned to the company for further preservation work in accordance with its objectives. Capital is raised by means of gifts, loans or grants from private individuals, local authorities, central government or any other supportive body.

The limit of the liability of a member can be a token sum. Without such a limit members could find themselves in financial difficulties, even as a result of decisions in which personally they have played no active part. The effect of limited liability is to require, in the event of dissolution following the realisation of the trust's assets, a contribution not exceeding the specified amount from each member, and in some circumstances each ex-member who resigns within twelve months prior to the date of dissolution, towards any outstanding debt or liabilities incurred by the company.

The annual return should include the following:

1 The address of the registered office
2 Details of directors, including any other directorships
3 Any financial liabilities, including mortgages
4 The name and address of the company secretary (firm of solicitors, accountants, chartered secretaries, etc)
5 A copy of the certified accounts

The company must keep proper books of account, audited by a qualified auditor who has been appointed by members at the annual meeting. The form of the accounts is laid down by the Companies Acts and they must be circulated to members in advance of the company's obligatory annual meeting.

Because a company is a legal entity, a preservation trust which is also registered as a company may find it easier to raise finance for its operations. The strict legal requirements of a registered company contribute towards confidence that a trust is being soundly managed.

Covenants

The word 'preservation' in the title of a trust has particular significance when its charitable status is under scrutiny. It is important to be able to demonstate that it can continue to control the well-being of a restored building after its disposal, and that the building will be maintained unaltered for a considerable period. In the absence of covenants, a trust may be powerless to prevent new owners from altering a building beyond recognition or even from pulling it down. In such a case, the trust would merely have carried out a temporary restoration, and restoration has not so far been considered in law a charitable object.

To remain effective in second and subsequent freehold sales of a property, covenants need to be negative in character. The purpose of a negative covenant is to prevent owners carrying out certain specified works, such as installing new windows of a different design and materials from the originals. A covenant of this type can be passed down a chain of successive owners, whereas a positive covenant, imposing obligations on owners to undertake or make payment for works, cannot be passed down a chain. A positive covenant, being only valid between the original parties to a sale, is of doubtful value over a long period. The control which a vendor of a freehold property can exercise over the long-term preservation of a building is therefore limited, and negative, in scope. For this reason, the Charity Commission generally prefers sale by lease to sale on a freehold basis. A lease can contain a clause ensuring the proper maintenance of the property as well as requiring the consent of the lessor to any alterations, and so include the element of positive control lacking in freehold sales.

In a limited number of situations involving buildings of outstanding importance, the National Trust or the National Trust for Scotland have powers to enforce covenants against successive owners (Section 8 of the National Trust Act 1937 and Section 7 of the National Trust for Scotland Act 1938). This they could consider in response to a request from a buildings preservation trust, providing for the preservation of the property into the future and in this way meeting the test of charitability. Where the property concerned had significance in relation to others, or to land, with which the National Trusts are already involved, or in Scotland is part of a group in which other properties have been restored by the Little Houses Scheme, a request for the enforcement of covenants is most likely to receive a sympathetic response. But the number of occasions when a National Trust covenant may be taken on buildings restored by preservation trusts will necessarily be severely limited because of the administrative burden assumed by the Trusts in enforcing their terms.

If neither leasehold tenure nor National Trust-controlled covenants are appropriate, a third method of safeguarding a trust's charitable status may be considered. By retaining a small piece of land, it is possible to effect a covenant with a purchaser for the benefit of the retailed land, to provide the required element of control over future use and works affecting the property being sold. Although to be binding on successive owners such covenants must be negative, they are more likely to be effectively enforced if the rights vested in a closely related piece of land, such as part of the garden, are linked firmly to the property being disposed of. In this way, it is possible to control alterations, changes of use, intensification of use as from a house into flats, colour schemes and other matters of a 'negative' nature.

Each of these three methods, if properly executed, should ensure on-going preservation and so meet the requirements of the Charity Commission/Inland Revenue regarding property disposals.

A fourth method, although not necessarily satisfying the test of charitability, can provide the trust with a direct control over the future of a property it proposes to sell. This can be done by including a sale condition that the new owner should give the trust the first option to purchase, at the prevailing market value, if he/she subsequently decides to dispose of the property. Being a positive covenant, it could not be imposed on a second purchaser, but re-purchase by the trust would enable it to draw up a new deed of covenant containing the same condition, and so on. If the trust decided not to re-purchase, it could still ask that a similar condition to the one included in the first sale should be part of the second. In this way, a chain of covenants would be built up, but the safest way to ensure that the chain is not broken is for the trust itself to re-purchase and find its own new purchaser each time the current owner wishes to sell.

The Memorandum of Association

This is one of two parts of a trust's constitution, setting out its name, address, objects, limitations, the liability of its members, the means of disposal of its property on dissolution, and the keeping of accounts.

NAME

The name should clearly indicate the purpose of the trust and the geographical area in which the purpose is to be carried out. Some combination of the words 'historic buildings', 'buildings preservation' and 'preservation' is normal. The geographical area should not be drawn too tightly, especially in the case of trusts centred on small towns, when the words 'and district' are useful in enabling them to take an interest in properties beyond the town boundary. The word 'limited' should be included if the Memorandum limits members' liability. It must be included in the case of a company limited by guarantee.

OFFICES

The location of the registered office need only be in general terms (England, Scotland, Wales or Northern Ireland) though it can be more specific if preferred. Where the trust is also a registered company, the annual return must include the full address.

OBJECTS

If the trust is a company, its objectives must be set out in the Memorandum. If it is also a charity, the objects clause in the Memorandum will constitute the principal test as to its charitable purposes. The objects should refer to the preservation of land and buildings of architectural or historic interest or of special beauty, for the benefit of the people in the area of the trust's operations. A phrase such as 'or of special beauty' widens the trust's scope, if it wishes, to include properties additional to those included in the statutory lists compiled by the DoE. This constitutes the primary part of the objects clause.

The secondary part of the clause should define the powers of the trust to further that object, including its powers to acquire and dispose of land and buildings. The disposal clause should be sufficiently flexible to enable the trust to sell the freehold, let on lease or tenancy, exchange, mortgage or otherwise dispose of buildings or land. There should be no requirement to sell or not to sell property. The trust should have the power to exercise its own discretion in acquiring and disposing of property taking into account local circumstances. The power to carry out works, either on acquired property or as an agency on behalf of an owner, should be included together with the authority to acquire and dispose of furniture and equipment. The trust may also wish to issue publications both in the interest of conservation generally and in order to gain publicity and support for its own work.

The ability to raise money to finance its operations by means of subscriptions, donations, bequests, grants, mortgage and other loans and general fund-raising events is a key secondary object. The right to borrow money on such terms as the trustees think fit and the right to invest should be included. As well as the power to raise money, it should be able to make grants or loans to individuals, authorities or other bodies wishing to carry out preservation work. The Hampshire Buildings Preservation Trust Ltd is one that acts largely in the capacity of a safety net, offering grants or loans, making professional advice available and by carrying out repairs on behalf of other owners to buildings it does not itself own. Co-operation with other bodies to achieve its principal purpose and the general facility to do any things necessary to the attainment of the trust's primary object are both useful powers.

LIMITATIONS

Although it is helpful to define objects with a view to maximum flexibility, certain exclusions are necessary to meet charitable and limited company requirements. The Memorandum should state that the trust exists only for those charitable objects listed in the objects clause. It should be excluded from using any of its funds for any trade union objects as these are different from those of charitable trusts. Payment of any dividend or bonus to members of the trust should be specifically prohibited, but it may wish to give itself specific permission to pay interest on loans made by members. It may also wish to allow for payment for office accommodation owned by a member or payment of professional fees to a member who is not a trustee, although depending on circumstances it may be preferable to commission independent consultants. Since it is axiomatic that no trustee/director may benefit or appear to benefit financially from his/her trusteeship, no fees for services of any kind should be paid to trustees or to directors.

LIABILITY

Members of a trust could find themselves in personal financial difficulties if it fails and has to be wound up unless a limit is placed on the liability of members. This is achieved by a statement in the Memorandum to the effect that the liability of members is limited and by prescribing the extent, usually £1, of a member's liability.

DISPOSAL OF PROPERTY ON DISSOLUTION

The law requires that any property owned by the trust should, in the event of dissolution, be set against its debts and liabilities. Any balance left outstanding is available for charitable purposes only, such as some other charitable body with similar objects or, by agreement with the Charity Commission/Inland Revenue, some other charitable purpose.

KEEPING OF ACCOUNTS

Qualified auditors have to be appointed at the annual meeting to examine the books and certify that they are correct. Members must have the right of access to the accounts.

ALTERATIONS TO THE MEMORANDUM

If the trust is a registered charity, it is advisable for any alterations to the Memorandum of Association to be submitted at draft stage to the Charity Commission. Changes made without approval could possibly nullify the trust's charitable status.

The Articles of Association

The Articles of Association set out how the trust's purposes, defined in the Memorandum, are to be realised. They must be registered with the Memorandum and form the second part of the trust's constitution. The Articles must be in printed form and must be signed by the same persons who have subscribed to the Memorandum.

135

At the beginning the meaning of the words used in the text is set out, together with the title of relevant Acts of Parliament, the name of the trust, the title of its governing body, a reference to the registered office and seal and a definition of membership. Some trusts describe themselves as 'the Trust', others as 'the Company'. Some refer to the governing body as such or as 'the Council'. The terms 'director', 'member of the council' and 'member of the governing body' mean the same in practice.

MEMBERS

A company, including a trust operating as a company, may have members and is required to register the number of its members. Apart from individuals, provision may be made for local authorities or other appropriate bodies to become members, secured by the appointment of a representative of the authority or body. The view of the organisation concerned should be sought in advance.

Provision must be made for an annual general meeting of members in each calendar year. The AGM is the ultimate authority of the trust, to which the governing body is answerable. Other meetings, known as extraordinary general meetings, may be called by the governing body from time to time, or at the request of at least one-tenth of the members. Not less than twenty-one days' notice of the AGM and not less than fourteen days' notice of other general meetings must be given. At the AGM the governing body (executive committee, trust council, etc) is required to submit an annual report to the members and the audited accounts must be presented for approval. New members must be elected to replace any retiring from the governing body, the auditors must be appointed and their remuneration fixed, but in addition the AGM should be an opportunity for a wide-ranging discussion on the trust/company's activities. To extend its knowledge and to make the meeting an attractive event for the membership as a whole, a visiting speaker or a film might be included.

The Articles should set out the number of members constituting a quorum, include provision for meetings to be adjourned if a quorum is not present and for the chair to be taken in the absence of the chairman or vice-chairman. Proxy voting should be allowed for and the method of appointing a proxy provided for in the Articles.

THE GOVERNING BODY

The governing body may be called a 'Council', 'Executive Committee', 'Board of Directors' or any other suitable descriptive title. The number of members of the governing body may be fixed or the upper and lower limits may be fixed. Certain office-holders may be provided for, such as president, chairman and vice-chairman, and representatives of other organisations like local authorities, civic or amenity societies. If a continuing independent view is sought, a clause can be included enabling a non-member to join the governing body.

The group of people who first initiated the trust may become the first members of the governing body. Generally, the period of office is three years, with one-third of the members retiring annually and being eligible for re-election. Election must be by members, although the governing body may make a recommendation, and members' nominations. The consent in writing of a nominee is required.

RESPONSIBILITIES OF THE GOVERNING BODY

Part of the Articles of Association will set out how the governing body will run the affairs of the trust. One of its most useful powers should be the authority to appoint committees to undertake particular aspects of its work, for example fund raising, within terms of reference which must be compatible with the Memorandum and Articles. It is the responsibility of the governing body to see that minutes of its meetings and at AGM and committee level are kept and proven by the chairman's signature. By law, the minute book must be open to inspection by members.

Day-to-day management should be vested in the governing body. It will need to possess the power to purchase or otherwise acquire suitable property. To avoid any suspicion of corruption, it may be thought desirable to limit its powers in respect of property owned by a member, or in which a member has a financial interest. This can be done by making such acquisitions authorisable only by the full membership.

To enable the trust to act with the speed that is sometimes necessary when acquiring property, the governing body should be authorised to raise or borrow money and to enter into contracts. It should also be able to institute legal proceedings to safeguard the trust's interests.

The procedure for revising the Memorandum and Articles, if this proves to be necessary in the light of experience, should be set out. This will need to be by special resolution of the membership at an extraordinary general meeting, carried by at least 75 per cent of the membership attending. The governing body should also have the power to make regulations concerning the conduct of its business, including the frequency of meetings, authority to sign cheques and documents and the appointment of professional advisers.

DISQUALIFICATION

Safeguards need to be built into the Articles to make possible the removal of a member of the governing body, should circumstances require it. These may be if a member:

1 becomes bankrupt;
2 becomes of unsound mind;
3 is convicted of an offence which would bring the trust into disrepute;
4 ceases to be a member of the trust;
5 is required to resign by resolution of a majority of fellow members;
6 gives one month's notice in writing of resignation.

But any member who is removed should have the right to be heard at the general meeting at which his/her removal is sought.

THE SECRETARY

The secretary is the key figure in the trust's administration. The main qualification is enthusiasm but this should preferably be combined with some degree of administrative skill and experience. He/she is bound to be involved with every transaction and the greatest care needs to be taken in the appointment.

The governing body should have the power to appoint or remove the secretary, and it should fix the period of the appointment and remuneration, if any. If the trust is prepared to pay the fees involved, a firm of solicitors or chartered secretaries may be employed for the routine work, but it may still be considered sensible to appoint an honorary secretary to deal with matters of general policy. A secretary who is also a member of the governing body should not receive any remuneration.

THE SEAL

The seal has to bear the name of the trust and is to indicate its authority to a purchase or a legal agreement. A resolution of the governing body is needed to authorise the fixing of the seal, at which two members should be present to witness that the document concerned has been properly sealed.

ACCOUNTS AND AUDIT

The Articles will prescribe that an account be maintained of all sums received and expended. In the case of smaller trusts, the office of secretary and treasurer are sometimes combined, but in most cases it is probably advisable to have a separate treasurer.

Sales and purchases of goods and property and the trust's assets and liabilities should all be recorded and be available for inspection at any time by members of the governing body and, by arrangement, by other members. The income and expenditure account and the balance sheet, the auditors' report and the annual report must be sent to every member and presented at the AGM.

Auditors must be appointed at the AGM. Their purpose is to maintain an independent check on the financial affairs of the trust and, in the case of a company, must be professionally qualified. Auditors are responsible to the membership as a whole and are entitled to have access to the books and to attend and be heard at meetings.

DISSOLUTION

The dissolution clause in the Memorandum is normally repeated in the Articles.

SUBSCRIBING THE DOCUMENTS

Seven or more persons must sign the Memorandum and Articles, unless the membership is limited to less than fifty, when two signatures are sufficient. Both documents must contain the same signatures and they must be witnessed. The signing effectively constitutes the application to be incorporated as a company or trust. The signatories are known as subscribers and it is worth taking some trouble over their identification, especially with trusts having high ambitions. Membership and financial backing may be more easily attracted if the subscribers are well-known people who are experienced in their own fields. The broader the range of interests represented by the subscribers the better, as this will reflect the several areas of specialised knowledge — legal, financial, historical, etc — on which the trust is likely to require advice. Above all, it is vital to identify a core of local people who care about conservation and are keen to get started with the trust's work.

Copies of draft Memorandum and Articles and further advice generally may be obtained from the Civic Trust.

8
THE ROLE OF
LOCAL AUTHORITIES

Whereas a buildings preservation trust is set up for a single, primary object, a local authority's interests cover a wide field prescribed by legislation. So, unlike trusts, the administrative framework of a local authority, although securely established, is not specifically designed to further building conservation which, when compared with good drains, refuse collection and housing the old and the homeless, may not rate highly in a council's list of priorities. How high it comes will depend on the interests and enthusiasm of the council's members and officers, and on public attitudes generally towards the local heritage.

A local authority may operate at different levels in respect of its built heritage. The district councils (in the metropolis the London boroughs) have a statutory duty to arrive at decisions on proposals submitted to them for alterations to buildings that are included in the DoE's list of buildings of architectural or historic interest. This is a passive role that cannot be avoided and is entirely dependent on the initiative of others. At another level, they and the county councils may provide direct encouragement to historic buildings repair work by making grants or loans available. Conservation areas may be designated in which conservation objectives take a higher priority. There is a considerable armoury of powers designed to protect the heritage which an authority may use if it so wishes. At a very different level, because the risks and potential rewards are far greater, a local authority may itself become directly involved, on the purchase, renovate and sell basis known as revolving funds, in the renovation of historic buildings. Two such local authority schemes have been described in Part I.

Working with buildings preservation trusts
The need for direct action of this kind will vary from place to place. If an established and active buildings preservation trust already covers a local authority's area but there is still a need for further work, or work on an increased scale, it may be sensible to support or co-operate with the existing trust rather than compete. Support may take the form of

140

grants or loans to specific projects put forward by the trust, or the injection of capital into the trust's general capital fund. In the latter case, the authority, depending on the amount of capital involved, may require some say in the running of the trust. Support can take the shape of a mutually agreed list of buildings urgently needing repair, and the agreement of the authority to take repairs notice action to either secure their repair or acquisition — in effect on behalf of the trust — for the purpose of repair. This has been found to be a particularly effective method of precipitating repair work and usually achieves the repairs without further involving the trust. The knowledge that the trust is available to take over the building concerned enables the local authority to serve its repairs notice without fear that, if the owner fails to comply with the notice, it could be saddled with a building for which it has no use or means of repairing.

None of this would prejudice the charitable status of the trust, as co-operation between charities and local authorities is provided for in section 12 of the Charities Act 1960, and this can extend, in the view of the Charity Commission, to partial funding. At draft stage the buildings preservation trust will need to check any proposed arrangements with the Commission. Depending on the extent of co-operation, both parties may need to enter into a formal agreement dealing with such matters as the definition of their respective functions and liabilities, the financial contribution of each, the division of any proceeds of sale, insurance and non-completion. The division of the proceeds of sale could be on the basis of the proportion of funds put into the project, but a trust utilising volunteer labour may seek some recompense for its work in addition to the *pro rata* share reflected by funding. The local authority must accept that the consent of the Charity Commission (Inland Revenue in Scotland) would be required to the sale of the restored property and that they would wish to see both the realisation of the best possible price for the property and the imposition of adequate preservation covenants. Whether or not a trust is particularly active, the overlap of interests between the two bodies is alone sufficient to justify an approach to the trust secretary about the possibilities of co-operation. If a trust has been inactive, this may be just what is needed to get a programme of work under way.

Revolving funds

In other places it may be desirable for a local authority to initiate a revolving-fund scheme itself. There are two alternative methods. One is for the authority to set up its own charitable trust for the area it covers. To achieve charitable status and the advantages that flow from it, the trust would need to be independently administered and, even if local authority members make up the majority of the governing body, it should include an effective representation of non-council interests, such as local civic, amenity or historical societies. If those outside organisations contribute funds, increased representation may be justified. The objects of a local authority-inspired trust and the means by which it pursues those objects are similar to those of a trust initiated privately. Advice from the Charity Commission at an early stage might help to avoid unforeseen pitfalls. Once in being, the trust may be able to call on the professional skills of the local authority as circumstances permit or as may be appropriate, or it may choose to seek independent professional advice. It will be eligible for assistance from the AHF, and it will be in a good position to make a general appeal for financial assistance, preferably in order to add to a pump-priming endowment from the local authority. Two or more local authorities could, if they wished, act jointly to set up a buildings preservation trust covering the areas concerned.

The Hampshire Buildings Preservation Trust operates in this way. It was established in 1975 and has a board of management comprising six county councillors, three persons nominated by the county council, three nominated by the district councils and three by amenity societies in the county. It had the initial encouragement of over £100,000 working capital donated by the county council, which provides professional services to the trust free of charge. Its activities in its first eight years increased its capital to approximately £¼ million.

The second method is for the council to set up a local authority-administered revolving fund over which it has complete control. It will need to be funded for the most part by the council, and as such may become a victim of cut-backs at times of financial restraint, but it can provide a direct and satisfying practical dimension to the authority's planning policies and thereby secure a permanent place in its wide programme of work.

Before any formal proposal is considered, some groundwork is necessary. One or other of the grant-making trusts could be sounded out as to the possibility of capital grant or loan assistance — a positive response would immediately put the idea in a favourable light. The scope for the type of work envisaged, the needs of the market, likely grant aid from the Historic Buildings and Monuments Commission and the wider benefits — social, public image and job creation — should be considered. It will be helpful to members and officers who are not familiar with this type of work to know the purpose of the proposed revolving fund, the type of project that could be undertaken, how long it would take to complete, at what order of capital cost, whether a profit, loss or neither is envisaged, in which places the market prospects are best and the architectural and social needs greatest, and to be told of the experience of other authorities that have carried out similar work. An indication of support from local amenity groups, particularly if this amounts to practical help — for example in assisting with the manning of exhibitions describing projects — is likely to be persuasive. Even if the work is to be controlled by the council, it will be reassured and encouraged if it can be given firm evidence of support from outside, and if it can be shown that its efforts are likely to be appreciated.

Just as a core of people needs to be assembled to take the initiative before a buildings preservation trust can be set up, so it will be helpful to identify those members and officers most likely to sympathise with the objectives of a council-run revolving fund, particularly if they occupy key positions in the areas of the council's administration most affected — finance and planning. Membership of a local amenity society should be one indication of a positive response. Discussions with perhaps three or four key individuals of this type will ensure a well-informed core of support for the proposal when the time comes for it to be formally launched and compete with other demands on the authority's time and resources. A small group can exert an influence well beyond its numbers if it is knowledgeable and enthusiastic. In the case of authorities where there is the prospect of alternating party political control, it is useful to have cross-party representation amongst the members in the supporting group.

The framework for the proposed revolving fund should then be fed into the authority's management structure. At this stage, at least one officer and one member in a position of influence should be involved and a brief report on the proposal, including the names of the supporting members, should normally be discussed with the council's chief officer concerned with planning and conservation, if he/she has not previously been a party to the idea. It will probably be his/her task or that of the principal conservation officer to present the proposals to the chief officers. They will consider the report in the light of the council's overall responsibilities, and comment on or make recommendations about the allocation of required funds for consideration by the council's appropriate committees and ultimately by the full council.

How much of this early groundwork is carried out by the authority and how much by outside persons or interests will depend on local circumstances. Some authorities may well initiate the proposal themselves in-house and require little or no prompting from outside. This is much the best way as it provides the best hope for general council support. But the most enthusiastic members should always be kept well briefed. The scheme will be in competition with other ideas of how to allocate the council's resources, and it is possible that the programme of work will include one or two contentious projects that will require particular support.

9

THE FIRST PROJECT

Most trusts and councils that operate revolving funds have started cautiously, with a modest scheme or one in an area commanding good resale values. Normally, it will be of the greatest importance that the first scheme should be successful both architecturally and financially, as this will inspire confidence and keenness to tackle further work. Since the principal purpose of a council-operated revolving fund is similar to the primary object of a buildings preservation trust, it follows that architectural success must have the top priority — without this there is little purpose in setting up the fund. Financial success is relative. The properties to be renovated will often be those that normal market demand has left high and dry. It would be surprising, although not unknown, if commercial levels of financial success could be achieved with these properties. Financial success for a first revolving-fund scheme can legitimately be claimed when the proceeds of sale equal the capital cost, so that the council or trust can show that the benefits of the project to the street or area, and to the local heritage of historic buildings, have been realised at no cost. A modest profit to put back into the fund to help with difficult future schemes is desirable, but not essential.

Because residential market values can differ between one town and another and between streets in the same town, even for similar properties, a little time should be spent in finding out the approximate going rates in different places. The district valuer, who is an officer of the Inland Revenue, or the county valuer may be able to give advice to a local authority or a quick check can be made of asking prices by a look at estate agents' windows and property advertisements in the local papers. Bearing in mind that renovation costs are likely to be similar, except only in extremely remote locations, wherever the project may be the information about market values should quickly limit the range of alternatives. Since resale potential for uses other than residential is generally more difficult to predict, these areas may best be avoided for the first project.

With a suitable property or group of properties identified, probably but not necessarily listed buildings, the method of acquisition must be considered. The experience of Essex County Council and Suffolk Coastal District Council revolving funds suggests that the local authority's compulsory powers of acquisition are unlikely to be needed, as the properties may well have been on the market for some time and interest in purchase will probably be welcomed. Occasionally, there may be a reluctant vendor. If the property is listed, council repairs notice procedure may be followed, but as this could lead to several months' delay, it should be avoided if at all possible in the first project and left until later on in the fund's programme when the process of acquisition can be taking place while other work is going ahead. In the case of local authorities, property negotiations are normally dealt with by the county council's own valuer at county level and at district level by the district valuer acting on behalf of the district council.

Suitably experienced architects will need to be briefed to prepare a scheme for the repair and perhaps conversion of the property. The process of selecting an architect and quantity surveyor is described later. The next stages of the work, the preparation of a detailed scheme, obtaining tenders for the building work and the building stage itself, are mainly the responsibility of professional advisers, but for council schemes a liaison officer should be nominated to ensure that the work proceeds according to plan, to help with any difficulties and to report back to the council members. Depending on the size of the scheme, it may be considered desirable to suggest a small group of trust or council members whose job is to regularly monitor progress. It is important to keep members fully informed, particularly as the work is bound to attract public interest. It is equally important that there should not be undue alarm at the sometimes unwelcome and costly discoveries that will probably be made about the condition of the property as the work proceeds — the contract price should include contingency sums and normally there is good news to report as well as bad, but the process can be unnerving.

The need for profitable schemes

Different organisations have different methods of calculating income and expenditure accounts — one local authority may charge staff time, interest on capital and overhead costs whereas another may not, and a loss to one could show in the accounts as a profit to another. But whichever basis is used, profit or loss is one of the vital statistics of both trust and local authority schemes and an important influence on their management.

Profits, in this context never ends in themselves, have two main functions. For a newly set-up trust or local authority revolving fund, a profit on the first project is confidence-building. It demonstrates that the tangible benefits of the project have been obtained at no cost and with something in hand. It wins support from the uncommitted and helps to launch the scheme on a note of success. Once the scheme is launched, a policy of planning for an agreed ratio of profitable projects enables these to subsidise some that are bound to make losses. Among these can be some of the buildings most deserving of renovation and with the greatest spin-off benefits to the town concerned.

In the interests of the work of the fund as a whole, every opportunity should therefore be taken to carry out profit-making schemes, even if this involves competing with commercial firms carrying out similar work. The profit can never, of course, be guaranteed. The lesson of many projects is that, when completed, they attract a higher market value than had been originally anticipated, but the reverse is always possible. If, by a combination of good fortune and shrewd planning, the preservation trust's or the local authority's fund can be topped up from time to time with a profitable scheme, it will then be better able to tackle the really difficult buildings that may otherwise be left to fester unattended.

10
FINANCE

Grant-making trusts

The grant-making trusts cover a wide field of which building conservation is only a small part. Some have interests in specific fields, like religion, medicine or science; some apply their funds for general purposes; others restrict their interest to geographical areas. Because the benefits of renovation work can extend beyond the purely architectural aspects to other considerations — perhaps educational or social — the selection out of over 2,000 grant-making trusts of the most appropriate trust or trusts to approach requires personal knowledge in this field, suitable advice or careful study. A reference to the *Directory of Grant-making Trusts* published by the Charities Aid Foundation (48 Pembury Road, Tonbridge, Kent TN9 2JD) is a useful first step. It should be available in the local public library and contains a classification of charitable purposes, a list of trusts under the classification, a register containing detailed information about the trusts, a geographical and an alphabetical index of trusts and an alphabetical index of subjects. For organisations intending to carry out a programme of work, a copy of the directory would be a sensible investment.

About half the trusts possess an income of below £10,000 per annum and only fifty-five an income in excess of £1 million (1983 Directory). Assistance may be in the form of an outright grant, an interest-free or a low-interest loan or perhaps a guarantee against loss up to a specified amount, depending on the policy of the trustees. An interest-free loan and a grant, both from the Pilgrim Trust were influential in establishing Essex County Council's revolving fund and the NTS's Little Houses Scheme. Both were pump-priming amounts rather than large capital sums and illustrate the important snowball effect that can result from even modest assistance. This is an aspect that may be persuasive when trusts are approached for assistance.

The demands made on the trusts' resources commonly outstrip their capacity to respond, so it is essential to spend time on a carefully considered approach to the trusts that appear most suitable. The following steps are suggested:

1   Identify which of the trusts appear most likely to help in the area and for the purpose concerned and have the resources sufficient for the amount of help envisaged.
2   Identify the person to whom the request should be directed.
3   Provide the organisation's name, address, etc, and the name of a person for the trust to reply to.
4   Provide information about the administrative structure of the organisation.
5   Describe the purpose of the organisation, explain why the work it does is needed and what would be achieved by the project for which assistance is requested.
6   If it has already completed projects, describe them and how it intends to develop its work in the future.
7   As accurately as possible, set out the project's budget and timetable, explain how the funds will be raised, used and managed, giving details of other contributors and the incidence of costs if they are spread over more than one year (this enables the trusts to plan ahead).
8   Indicate the amount that is being asked for, when it will be needed and in what form (grant, loan, etc).
9   Describe procedures for controlling expenditure.
10 Provide sufficient information for the trust, bearing in mind that it will probably be unfamiliar with the scheme, to be able to assess its importance both in itself and to the area. A report in the form of a feasibility study, some photographs or outline plans will be helpful but too much information at the initial approach stage should be avoided — it can prove indigestible and further information can always be provided if requested.
11 Provide a copy of the organisation's latest accounts and of any printed matter.

The application should be signed by an appropriate officer of the organisation, such as its secretary or chairman, and the grant-making trust should be informed if the person concerned is available for interview.

A list of grant-making trusts is given in the Appendix.

Commercial interest

Perhaps the outstanding feature of the impressive achievements in Amsterdam of the company known as Town Restoration Ltd (Stadscherstel) is that it destroyed the false barriers between conservation and commercial interests. So have the activities in the USA of the Historic Savannah Foundation. The founder of the Amsterdam company was a businessman, a director of a city brewery, who believed it was necessary to interest major commercial companies in restoration if work was to proceed on the scale and at the rate needed. He persuaded nine insurance companies, two banks and two shipping companies to contribute an initial share capital equivalent to about £250,000. Twenty-five years later there were fifty shareholders, including the City of Amsterdam, with a capital of £7 million. Additionally, it has £1 million of mortgage capital, put up by the thirteen original contributors. To the Amsterdam company, restoration is art and business combined. Although the organisations involved expected only a modest financial return on their basically secure property investments, they had the satisfaction of helping in the improvement of the city and they were each recipients of the public goodwill that followed.

The problem facing Savannah in 1964 was a considerable, but disregarded, heritage. With credit from a consortium of banks and some private contributors, a revolving fund was established to help improve some of the 1,100 city centre properties identified as being of architectural interest. Again with the help of local banks, a separate organisation was established specifically to make low-rental residential accommodation available — the banks recognised this as a way of developing a healthy and stable community. In Savannah, conservation involves the city, its institutions and its commerce, and success is measured in economics as well as history and bricks and mortar. The improvement of properties has led to a rise in property values, city revenues have increased, the return of a resident population to declining areas has boosted internal trade and the $100 million annual tourist income (1982) is twice the annual payroll of Savannah's largest industrial complex. As the president of the Historic Savannah Foundation, Lee Adler, pointed out:

> In 1960 a 4 storey, stucco-over-brick house in Gordon Row could be bought for $2,500. Today, one is around $85,000, unrestored when you can find and buy one — quite an investment. I spent over 20 years as a stockbroker and I can tell you that IBM has risen only sevenfold in that time. Restoration has been even a better investment than Coca-Cola stock!

Both the Amsterdam Company for Town Restoration Ltd and the Historic Savannah Foundation speak the language of finance and business as much as that of conservation, and this must assist when it comes to persuading commercial organisations to lend their support. Likewise, the chief fund-raiser responsible for establishing the Civic Trust's Architectural Heritage Fund as an effective conservation weapon in the UK is the senior partner in a firm of city accountants. Knowing the ropes helps; particularly if the commercial organisation concerned has not before been involved in this field, or is sceptical about the benefits it could bring.

150

Trusts or councils approaching commerce for support can point to the advertising potential and public goodwill a project might entail, but a fully considered financial plan is essential to establish credibility. As part of an RIBA research study into revolving funds (1982–3), one of the clearing banks gave the following guidelines as to its line of enquiry in the event of an approach for aid from a buildings preservation trust:

1 Is the trust a properly constituted charity with full powers to undertake the prescribed operation free of all capital and income taxes?

2 What are the trust's capital resources and what funds are its members prepared to allocate to the project under review?

3 Has a firm price been agreed for the purchase of the land/property and have all necessary consents been obtained for the redevelopment/preservation?

4 Are all sources of grants and alternative funding secure?

5 Have estimates for the construction work been obtained? Can fixed-price tenders for the building and ancillary trades be negotiated?

6 Has a firm timescale for the project been established and has the outflow of payments been fairly precisely determined?

7 Is it possible to reconcile the outflow of funds with the grants and other funding inflow to produce a detailed cash-flow forecast to demonstrate the level and timing of the bank's support required?

8 Have all interest accruing and professional costs been fully allowed for in the cash-flow forecast, based on a conservative estimate of the time required to achieve a sale or lease, etc?

9 At which stage is a buyer likely to be sought? Has a professional view been obtained regarding the value of the completed project and the prospects for attracting an early buyer?

10 How is any shortfall on sale beyond the resources of the trust to be funded? And where these relate to fund-raising activities are the plans realistic?

11 What security is available to the bank? On the assumption that it remains the policy of the AHF to protect the fund by taking a mortgage over the property concerned, the bank is likely to expect security by:
   a) a second mortgage over the property and/or
   b) members' guarantees.

A bank may be prepared to adjust its normal commercial criteria and give special assistance to trusts. This assistance may include: adjusting the ratio between its support and self-generated funds; fine interest rates determined by its assessment of the risk factor and/or its particular view of the project; the waiving of all commitment fees; and the level of security required falling short of its normal margins.

If there is a clearly identified shortfall of income over outgoings, a bank may be prepared to make a donation, though it will not wish to enter into an open-ended commitment. Its decision is likely to be based upon:

1   Its representation in the area.
2   The level of its support for other local community projects past and present.
3   The nature of the redevelopment/preservation.
4   The ultimate beneficiary of its contribution.
5   The extent of its perceived contribution through the normal financing operation.

A combination of a favourably structured bridging advance with a donation may enable some projects to be undertaken which would otherwise not be feasible. With regard to council-operated projects, a borrowing facility at the bank would be expected to reflect the risk-free status of the authority and would be negotiated at fine commercial rates. A bank's criteria for assessing a local authority's appeal for a donation towards a project are likely to be as above.

The scope for greater participation by building societies may be increased by forthcoming legislation, but there is no reason why a society should not provide loans on the security of the property being improved if there is sufficient value in the property to enable the loan to be made, and if the society is satisfied as to the status of the borrower and has the funds in hand. Depending on prevailing rates of interest, this may or may not be attractive. It would also seem to be in order for a building society to respond to a modest appeal for funds, as long as some publicity is given to the name of the society so that expenditure can be deemed to be advertising.

Whereas nine insurance companies formed the backbone of the Amsterdam company's initial appeal for funds, the RIBA study indicated a cautious attitude governing and limiting the participation in similar work of the five UK insurance companies that provided information. Soundings by the British Insurance Association of some of its members produced a similar impression. In the UK, it is the banks that have figured most prominently in providing finance for historic building conservation but, as the Bradford-on-Avon project in Market Street shows, persistence in asking is a virtue. The public relations, phoenix-like aspect of the work appears to provide good material for commercial exploitation.

Guarantors
There are too many uncertainties for the financial outcome of a renovation scheme to be forecast with great accuracy, and this may deter some from proceeding, even though the records appear to show more that are financially successful than otherwise. Even professional advisers who

would like to see a scheme proceed may well adopt a cautious approach; they may be congratulated on a better-than-forecast result but they will almost certainly be criticised for one that is poorer than forecast. A system of guarantors could remove the uncertainty, ensure a break-even position and enable even an apparently loss-making scheme to proceed.

The guarantor could be a large commercial organisation, a local businessman or a private individual. (Official organisations tend to prefer grants or loans as this way they know the money will be spent, rather than provide a guarantee which may or may not be spent.) Each may have reasons for wishing to see a scheme proceed: as a nearby resident or shopkeeper, to see the street or area improved perhaps, or, as an owner of a facing or adjoining property, in the expectation of seeing the market value of their own property rise when the scheme is completed.

Although commercial organisations seem to have only rarely taken advantage of the possibilities, proposals resulting in the improvement of what may often have been a notorious local eyesore that has blighted the neighbourhood for years are bound to attract interest and publicity. They are likely to be a talking point in the area, and perhaps beyond, from the time ideas are first made public to completion, for probably two years or more. A guarantor can receive sustained, favourable publicity and, since the financial outcome is frequently better than originally anticipated, may well not be called upon to provide the indemnity guaranteed.

Likely sources of support should be identified and approached when proposals are at a draft stage.

The livery companies
The livery companies are City of London institutions, historically connected with the trades of the city. They now number over ninety. The companies having a field of interest most related to building and allied work are listed in the *Conservation Sourcebook* published by the Crafts Advisory Committee, 12 Waterloo Place, London SW1Y 4AN. Where projects involve the preservation of a building directly connected with one of these trades or where part of the work, particularly if it is of a specialised nature, has such a connection, a livery company may be interested in supporting the project; for example, the Masons Company supports the conservation of the heritage of fine stone buildings and the Ironmongers has assisted with the restoration, preservation or provision of examples of craftsmanship in iron. The addresses of the livery companies may be obtained at any local reference library. Similar care

and preparation as in making an application to the grant-making trusts should be taken. A list of livery companies is given below:

The livery companies in order of precedence (1982)

Mercers (textiles)	Cooks	Needlemakers
Grocers	Coopers (cask makers)	Gardeners
Drapers	Tylers and bricklayers	Tinplate workers
Fishmongers	Bowyers (bow makers)	Wheelwrights
Goldsmiths	Fletchers (arrow	Distillers
Merchant Tailors	makers)	Pattern makers
Skinners (Furriers)	Blacksmiths	Glass sellers
Haberdashers	Joiners	Coachmakers and
Salters	Weavers	Coach Harness
Ironmongers	Woolmen	Makers
Vintners	Scriveners (drafters of	Gunmakers
Clothworkers	documents)	Gold & Silver Wyre
Dyers	Fruiterers	Drawers
Brewers	Plaisterers (plasterers)	Makers of Playing
Leathersellers	Stationers &	cards
Pewterers	Newspaper makers	Fanmakers
Barbers	Broderers	Carmen
Cutlers	(embroiderers)	Master Mariners
Bakers	Upholders	Solicitors
Wax Chandlers	(upholsterers)	Farmers
Tallow Chandlers	Musicians	Air Pilots and Air
Armourers	Turners	Navigators
Girdlers	Basketmakers	Tobacco Pipe Makers
Butchers	Glaziers	Furniture Makers
Saddlers	Horners (makers of	Scientific Instrument
Carpenters	horn spoons, etc)	Makers
Cordwainers	Farriers	Chartered Surveyors
(shoemakers)	Paviors	Chartered Accountants
Painter Stainers	Loriners (spur-makers)	Chartered Secretaries
Curriers (leather	Apothecarers	& Administrators
dressers)	Shipwrights	Builders' Merchants
Masons	Spectacle Makers	Launderers
Plumbers	Clockmakers	Marketors
Innholders	Glovers	Actuaries
Founders	Feltmakers	Insurers
Poulterers	Framework Knitters	Arbitrators

Local authority grants

The availability of local authority grant assistance fluctuates in response to cash allocation and expenditure limits decided at central government level, and also by priorities determined by the individual authorities. There are two main categories of grants: those made under the Housing Acts for home improvement and related works, and those made under the Town & Country Planning Acts for conservation schemes, usually involving historic buildings.

HOME IMPROVEMENT GRANTS

There are four main types of grant but only one, intermediate grant, is mandatory. Intermediate grants cover the provision of basic facilities such as inside WCs, bathrooms and hot and cold water supplies where these amenities do not exist. Repairs, improvement and special grants are made at the discretion of the local authority. Repairs grants can be made for comprehensive schemes of repair to pre-1919 houses. Improvement grants are for major works to houses in particularly poor condition. Special grants are for properties in multi-occupation where amenities are shared. Intermediate and improvement grants apply to houses built or converted before 1961. In Scotland, improvement grants for properties in Housing Action Areas are mandatory.

Listed buildings qualify for increased levels of repair and improvement grants, depending on their grade. A detailed guide to improvement grants is provided in 'Home Improvement Grants: A Guide for Home-Owners, Landlords and Tenants', which is available free of charge from HMSO and from local authorities.

GENERAL IMPROVEMENT AREAS

Where whole groups or streets of run-down houses need attention and there is a need to improve the general setting and environment, local authorities may designate general improvement areas (GIAs). In these the availability of housing improvement grants is promoted and funds may also be available for external works such as repaving and tree planting. Since long-lasting improvement must often embrace more than buildings alone, the latter can have particular value.

CONSERVATION SCHEMES

Under this heading there are a variety of permutations of local authority grant aid. None is mandatory and consequently availability differs widely from authority to authority. Assistance may be in the form of loans or, more usually, cash grants based on a percentage of the cost of the work proposed. Retrospective applications are not eligible.

Aid to listed buildings is perhaps the type of assistance that is most common, but some authorities apply their resources to a specific building type, such as churches, and some to repairs to buildings in conservation areas. Others take advantage of joint schemes known as Town Schemes in which the authority and the Historic Buildings and Monuments Commission (HBMC) formally agree a fixed amount which each will make available for a period, usually three years, for repairs to a selected list of buildings in a conservation area. The scheme is promoted by the local authority in the area concerned. Sometimes informal joint funding arrangements are made between an authority and the commission.

Since the scope of grant aid from local authorities is wide but availability is generally unpredictable, enquiries must be made at the appropriate departments of the local authority to ascertain the position in a particular area.

DoE grants

Under the headings of urban programme grants, urban initiatives fund, city partnerships and derelict land grants, the DoE channels funds to the regions for work that can sometimes include historic buildings renovation and the restoration of derelict sites. Funds are passed mainly through the local authorities, but also in some cases, such as derelict land grants, to individuals and professional and voluntary groups (see Chapter 12 of Part II: Feasibility Studies). From time to time new schemes are introduced and old ones are phased out. Initial enquiries should be directed to the local authority concerned or to the DoE, 2 Marsham Street, London SW1P 3EB, or to the Scottish Development Agency, 120 Bothwell Street, Glasgow G2 7JP.

Historic Buildings and Monuments Commission (English Heritage)
Historic Buildings Council for Scotland
Historic Buildings Council for Wales

From 1 April 1984 English Heritage, an independent Commission, took over the work in England previously carried out as part of the DoE by the Historic Buildings Council for England. In Scotland and Wales the equivalent organisations to the former HBC continue to function under the jurisdiction of the respective Secretaries of State. One of the functions of the Commission and the Councils is the allocation of grant aid for historic buildings. This is done under four categories.

1 INDIVIDUAL BUILDINGS

Grants may be offered to buildings, both church and secular, considered to be of outstanding architectural or historic interest. Grants are made towards the cost of urgent major structural repairs such as reroofing, eradication of wet and dry rot, etc, but not for minor repairs, maintenance works or decoration. They are conditional upon repairs being carried out in a manner sympathetic to the character of the building and to the highest possible standards, using traditional materials wherever possible. A full specification and schedule of works must be approved before work starts. Other conditions relate to future works and ownership, and the provision of public access to the buildings. Owners have to show that they would not be able to complete the work without financial help and may be asked to supply details of assets and income to substantiate their application. Unless a building has been empty for some time and the applicant represents possibly the last chance for the building's survival or there are other special circumstances, grants are not offered for recently purchased properties as their state of repair is presumed to have been taken into account in the purchase price.

2 HISTORIC TOWNS AND AREAS
Town Schemes (see also under local authority grants)
These are designed to encourage the comprehensive repair of whole groups of properties. The properties which are eligible for assistance are agreed by the commission and the local authority, assistance being dependent on the suitability of the work and on the availability of funds. Some local authorities exclude certain categories of property, such as commercial, and there is a general policy excluding major companies and new purchases. Administration may be by the Commission or the local authority depending on whether or not the scheme is delegated.

Conservation areas
Although grants towards building repairs are theoretically obtainable in any conservation area, they are in practice limited on the following basis:

1　For works to a building in a conservation area of particular architectural or historic interest, for which the local authority has been invited by the commission to submit a programme of conservation work.
2　Where there is a town scheme in operation in the same part of the conservation area as the application site.
3　Where the work is part of a scheme of conservation work prepared by local authorities, amenity societies, preservation trusts or a group of private owners, for example a scheme for the restoration of buildings in a particular square, terrace, street or village. The individual grants sought could be for relatively small sums. To be accepted as a scheme, the total of the grants for the properties included in it must currently amount to £2,500 or more, ie £10,000 of work.

3 ANCIENT MONUMENTS

Grants may be made to private owners (or local authorities as appropriate) for the preservation and consolidation of ancient monuments. These grants broadly parallel the grants available for historic buildings.

4 OTHER WORK

Architectural structures — paths, walls, formal pools, etc — in historic parks and gardens may be eligible for grant aid.

For further information contact the local authority or, in England, English Heritage, 25 Savile Row, London W1X 2BT; in Scotland, Historic Buildings Council for Scotland, 25 Drumsheugh Gardens, Edinburgh EH3 7RN; and in Wales, Historic Buildings Council for Wales, Crown Buildings, Cathays Park, Cardiff CF1 3NQ.

The Architectural Heritage Fund

The establishment of the AHF was one of the specific aims of the UK Campaign for European Architectural Heritage Year 1975. Its capital comes partly from the government and partly from the private sector. Its purpose is to provide cheap additional working capital to supplement funds which preservation trusts raise from their own and other sources. By the end of 1984 loans made by the Fund had topped £3 million, of which approximately £1 million was represented by current contracts. The Fund is controlled by a council of management representing the DoE and the Civic Trust in equal numbers. Through the council's applications committee, decisions can be taken very quickly when necessary. The Civic Trust carries out day-to-day administration.

Loans are normally for not more than 50 per cent of the cost of a project (including, where appropriate, the cost of acquisition) and normally for a period of not more than two years. Interest is calculated at 5 per cent per annum for the agreed period of the loan and, should the capital not be repaid within that time, rises thereafter to the base rate of the National Westminster Bank, the Fund's clearing bank. In addition, where the building is to be resold after restoration, the Fund reserves the right to gear repayment of the loan to the selling price of the restored building; thus, for example, if the Fund advance 40 per cent of the cost of acquisition and restoration, the loan repayment would be calculated as 40 per cent of the selling price, but this geared repayment will never exceed the amount of the loan plus interest for the entire period of the loan at 3 per cent above the base rate of the National

Westminster Bank. In calculating any liability to profit-sharing under this formula, the Fund allows the gross cost of the project to be offset against sale proceeds, thus enabling the borrowing trust to retain the full benefit of grant aid.

If the building is to be resold after restoration, the fund protects its capital by taking a first charge on the property which is the subject of the loan. Where there is no intention to resell, a guarantee of repayment from a bank, local authority or some comparable corporate body is required.

Enquiries should be addressed to the Architectural Heritage Fund, Civic Trust, 17 Carlton House Terrace, London SW1Y 5AW.

National Heritage Memorial Fund

The fund gives financial assistance towards the cost of acquiring land and buildings of outstanding interest and of importance to the national heritage. Assistance for repair is only given in exceptional cases. The fund will need to be satisfied that there is no other source of help for the project or that its scale is such that additional funds are necessary. Assistance is only given to non-profit-making bodies, including local authorities, and is normally conditional on some form of access for the public.

Further information may be obtained from the National Heritage Memorial Fund, Church House, Great Smith Street, London SW1P 3BL.

Tourist boards

Where a project improves the amenities in an area, extends the holiday season or extends the use of an amenity and needs assistance to get started, grants or loans may be available from a tourist board. Projects must be substantially for the benefit of tourists and must be viable.

The basis of assistance is individual need, but the maximum for medium-sized projects is 25 per cent of the eligible cost and total assistance from this and other public sector funds combined must not exceed 50 per cent. In comprehensive or ambitious projects that may be phased over a period of several years, tourist boards may be interested in helping with specific parts of the project, such as a reception/shop area in a museum, particularly if it is designed to provide the scheme with an income.

Further information may be obtained from:

English Tourist Board, 4 Grosvenor Gardens, London SW1W 0DU

Scottish Tourist Board, 23 Ravelston Terrace, Edinburgh EH4 3EU
Wales Tourist Board, Brunel House, 2 Fitzalan Road,
  Cardiff CF2 1UY
Northern Ireland Tourist Board, River House, 48 High Street,
  Belfast BT1 2DS

Council for Small Industries in Rural Areas (COSIRA)

In certain rural areas of England, grants for converting redundant buildings into workplaces are available from the Development Commission through its agency COSIRA. The grants are intended primarily to provide employment for countryside communities, but can involve the renovation and conversion of any suitable redundant building, including barns, chapels, schools, railway stations, mills and factories.

Applications may be made by individuals, voluntary groups, trusts or companies. Converted buildings can be intended for use by applicants themselves or for leasing to others. In considering applications COSIRA has regard to the existing supply of business premises in the area concerned. Grants are based on a percentage of the costs of the repair and conversion work together with professional fees. Eligible items can also include the provision of heating, lighting, power and water supplies, drainage and access. Modest extensions may also be included. Applications must be supported by drawings and costings, and the normal statutory approvals must be obtained from the local authority. Any application must be made and approved before works commence.

The applicant is responsible for the design, supervision and completion of the works but help and advice is available from COSIRA at all stages. COSIRA can also assist in finding tenants. Further information about the grants and advice available can be obtained from local COSIRA offices.

Countryside Commission

Projects which have a bearing on the countryside, such as the restoration of the parkland setting of a country house or the provision of an information or interpretive centre, may qualify for assistance from the Countryside Commission. Like the more recently established English Heritage, the Commission is an independent statutory agency. It has the power to assist local authorities, private individuals, trusts and other groups by giving advice and grant aid. Most county authorities work closely with the Commission and may be contacted locally with enquiries. They will provide the address of the Commission's regional office. Alternatively, enquiries should be addressed to:

Countryside Commission, John Dower House, Crescent Place, Cheltenham, Gloucestershire GL50 3RA

Countryside Commission for Scotland, Battleby, Redgorton, Perth PH1 3EW

National Council for Voluntary Organisations (NCVO)

NCVO provides advice to voluntary groups wishing to undertake projects. In 1983, with DoE assistance, it published a community buildings project folder containing information under the headings of preparing and setting up a project, statutory requirements, conversion work, management and the role of local authorities. The folder also includes case studies of projects and comprehensive notes on funding sources, technical aid centres, how to choose an architect, references and useful contacts.

Further information can be obtained from: NCVO, 26 Bedford Square, London WC1.

Local fund raising

The Bradford-on-Avon Trust has demonstrated the potential of a comprehensively organised and sustained series of fund-raising events. A complete list of events together with the sums raised in aid of the Trust's project in Market Street, Bradford-on-Avon is shown on p162:

Although too much should not be read into individual results, some events were outstandingly successful and may provide a rough-and-ready guide to the prospect of similarly organised events elsewhere, particularly if they are based on the many facets of a small-town community like Bradford-on-Avon's.

Taking a wider area, fund raising may take on a different character. Since 1982 the Suffolk Historic Churches Trust's major annual fund-raising effort has been propelled on two wheels and gathering increasing momentum. In 1982 about 2,900 people took part in the bicycle ride and raised £58,000; in 1983 3,600 people raised £72,000. The 1984 ride raised £74,000 for Suffolk and the event was co-ordinated with others on the same day in Essex, Cambridgeshire, Lincolnshire and Norfolk. In 1985 Kent and Sussex got on their bikes. The sponsored bicycle ride is particularly suited to raising money for churches and chapels.

To achieve results of this order, a great deal of organisation and planning is required, starting at least six months in advance to make sure that the churches will be open for inspection in every parish in the county on the appointed day. To do this, a letter is circulated in December with the Diocesan Christmas mail. In January and February

1980–1		1981–2	
Donations	3,533.49	Donations	410.00
Coffee mornings	42.09	Antique fair	8.31
Folk festival	459.15	Bottle	61.58
Gardening advice	30.00	Coffee mornings	206.57
Launching party	978.57	Calendars sale	9.00
Market stall	554.78	Children's fashion show	198.00
Money in jar	111.53	Commission on pictures sold at Priory Barn	11.45
Musical evening	147.47	Dressmaking and dolls clothes	10.00
Nearly new	999.25	Fifty/Fifty auction	1,660.00
Pastry party	179.60	Film show	45.30
Plant sales	76.89	Gardening advice and sale of produce	52.55
Sewing and Cindy clothes	50.00	Guided tours of Bradford-on-Avon	50.90
Snowball lunches	307.00	Gardens open to the public	180.95
Sponsored bird watching	138.22	Market stall (held monthly)	356.28
Sponsored bicycle ride	445.47	Market stall (St Margaret's Hall)	65.00
Town tour	7.40	Nearly new	204.00
Wine tasting evening	203.40	Lectures	32.35
		Open day at Priory Barn	60.90
		Poetry evening	27.70
		Restoration of porcelain	5.00
		Sponsored walk	1,000.00
		Rugmaking	1.50
		Spinning profits	20.00
		Sponsored bicycle ride	185.63
		Sponsored bird watching	6.50
		Tupperware party	29.50
		Teas profit	114.52
		Tray making	20.00
		Cake making	12.55
		Miscellaneous less small expenses	6.32
TOTAL 1980–1	8,264.31	TOTAL 1981–2	5,052.36
		TOTAL 1980–2	£13,316.67

literature, publicity and printing are put in hand. Meetings with the Deanery area organisers are held in the spring at which briefs, guidance notes, parish return forms and sponsor forms are distributed. A master list of churches to be open is prepared and printed in June and July on the basis of an event in early September. The planning required is of military precision, and the local authority and the police should be notified. In 1984 658 churches, chapels and other places of worship promised to be open.

Not everyone used a bicycle — one teenager set out on foot, covering thirty miles and visiting twenty churches — but groups of walkers on roads are discouraged and motorised transport is permitted only to get to the first church and to go home from the last. Above all it is an enjoyable event; one eight-year-old wrote to her area organiser, 'We visited 33 churches and raised £85. We enjoyed a lovely day out and I am looking forward to the next ride.'

Significantly, perhaps, the sponsored walk in Bradford-on-Avon raised more than the bicycle rides. The system developed in Suffolk, taking advantage of existing organisational frameworks, has been shown to be admirably suited to fund raising for churches in a rural county. At a smaller scale or in an urban area a sponsored walk may be more appropriate and successful. The theme for the walk or the ride could change from year to year and the funds raised put either to a particular project or to a general capital fund.

Each local fund-raising campaign should be tailored to the resources of the organisers, the interests of local people and the character of the buildings in the area. It is a challenge to local imagination and ingenuity and has the valuable dual effect of raising money and of establishing the organisers' work as a community effort.

11
MANPOWER SERVICES COMMISSION

The Manpower Services Commission (MSC) is a government agency that, amongst other things, assists people who are seeking employment and/or training, and supports projects which meet these objectives and which are of benefit to the community. Under its Community Programme the MSC aims to provide temporary work for the long-term, adult unemployed whilst under its Voluntary Projects Programme the Commission provides the opportunity for voluntary work, possibly as a prelude to obtaining paid work. The detailed provisions for these schemes are subject to periodic revision so up-to-date information should be obtained from the MSC Employment Division area office.

The Community Programme
Any individual or organisation with suitable management resources can sponsor a project. Although the sponsor is expected to pay the local rate for the job, substantial help is given by the MSC towards the wages, including the employer's National Insurance contributions for each person employed. The wages of managers and supervisors are reimbursed in full, up to agreed limits, and those of other workers up to an average of £63 per week (1984) over the period of the project. The cost of agreed essential overheads, materials, professional advice, training and equipment can also be refunded, generally up to a maximum of £440 per year (1984) for each person employed, excluding managers and supervisors.

The main criteria for the inclusion of a project in the Community Programme are:

1 The work to be done must be of benefit to the community.
2 The primary object should be to provide jobs which can be filled by people who have been out of work for several months so as to help towards their long-term employment prospects.
3 Projects must involve work which would not otherwise be done.
4 The appropriate local wage should be paid to employees.
5 If the projects touch on the interests of trades unions or existing employers, the written support of the unions and the employer's federation should be obtained.

6   Projects must be financially sound in respect of any costs not met by the MSC.

7   Sponsors must have the ability to manage their projects and to take on the full responsibilities of an employer. (An agent, often a local authority, may undertake the administration of a project on behalf of the sponsor, which is then known as an associated sponsor.)

In the case of building and construction work, sponsors or their agents are responsible for obtaining all local authority consents and for ensuring that the work is carried out to an acceptable standard. Although the MSC may accept professional fees as part of a project's refundable operating costs, it will not pay fees incurred before the project is approved. Sponsors in the private sector must derive no personal gain from a project but they can benefit indirectly, such as in the fields of public image and publicity. However, benefits of this sort must be secondary to the benefits to the community.

Useful support to sponsors and projects may be obtained from Practical Action, an organisation funded jointly by the MSC, private firms and charitable trusts. Practical Action can provide management and professional advice, materials, equipment and secretarial and office services. It can also pass on the benefit of discounts on materials and equipment negotiated with major suppliers. Further information from Practical Action, 4th Floor, Victoria Chambers, 16–20 Scrutton Ground, London SW1P 2HP, or from the MSC area office.

The Community Programme has been operating since 1982 and a number of building refurbishment schemes have been assisted, including the Long Shop Museum at Leiston (see Chapter 1). Here the sponsor is a charitable trust headed by the Earl of Cranbrook. The interests represented by the trustees include farming, engineering and local government, while a retired insurance manager acts as secretary and treasurer and deals with day-to-day management and finance. Other projects assisted by the Community Programme have been the conversion of warehouses into a community centre, the renovation and conversion of a derelict farmhouse into a youth centre, and the ambitious scheme in Bristol for the conversion of the Old Station at Temple Meads into a national centre for engineering, involving an eighty-strong MSC-funded team. A full guide to Community Programme procedures is set out in the 'Sponsors and Agents Handbook', obtainable from MSC area offices, which can provide further general information.

Voluntary Projects Programme

This is designed to provide voluntary opportunities for unemployed people to help them prepare for and obtain paid work. The programme works through sponsors along similar lines to the Community Programme. The sponsor is responsible for the recruitment of volunteers, the allocation of funds supplied by the MSC and will need the management resources to design and administer a project, together with the financial resources to cover any expenses which cannot be funded through the programme itself. In addition to the voluntary helpers, paid employees may be recruited to help run projects if the sponsor is unable to do so. Paid employees must be recruited from the unemployed and the MSC reimburses sponsors for approved wages and employers' National Insurance contributions. Paid tutors/instructors may also be recruited on a part-time basis. Sponsors assume the responsibilities of an employer in respect of paid staff and in matters such as health and safety at work and insurance in respect of voluntary staff.

The approved costs must be agreed by the sponsor and the MSC before the project is started. Sponsors must make full use of existing resources, such as premises, but the MSC will meet costs up to a maximum of £75,000 (1984) for any single project. Approved costs may cover staffing, premises, materials and equipment, certain volunteers' expenses and general operating costs. A sponsors' handbook is available from area MSC offices.

The kind of projects undertaken will depend on the skills available to perform and supervise them, and the scope from area to area. The Voluntary Projects Programme might often be of assistance with clearance or landscaping elements of work on land closely related to a property renovation project or even with some elements, such as decorating, of a renovation scheme itself. Because the work is, for the most part, voluntary, project organisers should have suitable personality and drive and be able to pass on their enthusiasm to others.

12
FEASIBILITY STUDIES

Unless the potential of what may appear to be a poor and useless property can be spotted and demonstrated, it is unlikely ever to be realised. Feasibility studies, professionally undertaken and channelled towards those with the power to act, are a means of highlighting potential.

The local authorities should be best placed for an overall view of the problem in their own areas and they often possess staff with suitable qualifications and experience to carry out feasibility studies. If not, consultants can be commissioned but a local authority must, as always, consider this work against the background of the many other demands on its resources. Because of this, the helping hand of voluntary groups, either to assist the authority or to undertake the leading role, may be welcomed by many authorities. Voluntary groups may also decide to initiate feasibility studies, for which there are two sources of grant aid specifically for this purpose.

RIBA Community Projects Fund
Since 1982–3 the DoE has allocated funds to the RIBA for it to make small grants to voluntary organisations normally unable to afford professional advice so that they can undertake feasibility studies for building and other environmental projects. It is financed from the DoE's Urban Initiatives Fund. If the projects obtain capital funding, the money is returned to the RIBA for reuse.

In its first two years, half the projects aided have involved renovation and conversion work, spread evenly across the country, from large cities to small towns, rural areas and villages. Common to all is an attempt by local voluntary groups to reshape and improve the environment. Up to the end of 1984, sixty-six projects had received grant aid, including a scheme initiated and run by unemployed young people in Penzance to convert a derelict warehouse into a centre for social activities, the conversion of a disused railway shed in Broadbottom, on the edge of the Pennines, into a sports centre which includes an indoor riding school for the disabled, and the provision of low-cost office, workshop and studio accommodation in a vacant local authority-owned listed property in Cheltenham. Each of these schemes received a £500 pump-priming grant from the Fund.

Enquiries should be addressed to Community Projects Fund, RIBA, 66 Portland Place, London W1N 4AD.

Civic Trust

Aid for feasibility studies may also be available from the Civic Trust. For the first time in 1984–5, the Trust received a small grant from the DoE from its Urban Initiatives Fund, designed to enable local amenity societies, building preservation trusts and other voluntary groups in urban areas of England, actively involved in restoring derelict land or buildings, to obtain professional help.

The grants are to help to provide properly worked-out feasibility studies and plans at the early design and assessment of financial viability stage. The type of schemes eligible include architects' plans and working drawings, landscaping plans, quantity surveyor's cost analysis and an estate agent's or surveyor's valuation of the completed scheme's market price. Priority is given to projects in the inner city and in major urban areas. Enquiries as to current availability should be addressed to the Civic Trust, 17 Carlton House Terrace, London SW1Y 5AW.

13
DEPRESSED COMMUNITIES

Where dilapidation is the exception rather than the rule, improvement can be an isolated initiative, successfully achieving its object of removing an untypical blot on the street scene and encouraging others nearby to raise the standard of maintenance of their own properties to the general, prevailing level. But in many places there may be a need to improve, in addition to one or two isolated buildings, the whole image and morale of the area and its economic well-being. In such cases, individual renovation schemes may need to be part of a wider, more comprehensive programme of action based on the needs, wishes and support of local people, effective financial backing from central, local commercial and voluntary sources, the support of local government at all levels and the availability of knowledgeable advice wherever it is needed.

Involving local people
Unless the local community is involved, the results of any initiative to improve a depressed area are likely to be cosmetic and therefore short-lived. The standard public meeting may not be particularly effective in involving people — it is often more of a confrontation than a useful dialogue, an opportunity for a few people to let off steam after which everything returns to normal. Because traditional methods of public participation do not always produce the degree of involvement that is necessary in run-down areas, alternative techniques have been tried, with some success.

The use of town models to encourage interest and involvement by local people in the places in which they live has been pioneered by Dr Tony Gibson, Director of the Education for Neighbourhood Change Programme at the University of Nottingham. In this a basic, three-dimensional model of the place concerned forms the centre-piece of the public meeting, $1/2$ square mile occupying about a 6ft square. A variety of cut-out shapes, representing such things as pedestrian crossings, children's play areas, public toilets and community huts are available for people to arrange on the model in the places they feel they are needed. Anything that can be useful to the community can be included and if a cut-out is not already provided, blank cards can be used to fashion additional ones. Where this technique has been used, it has been found that it results in a useful process of discussion, ideas and rearrangement of the facilities that are considered to be lacking. When this has been done the professional advisers, up to then in the background, can comment on the legal, financial and technical possibilities and limitations.

The model technique serves without commitment, to explore possibilities and pool ideas. It also serves to break down the barriers in the traditional platform-and-audience relationship, since everyone gathered around the model, perhaps 15ft or more square, is on an equal footing. Personalities, which can be a hindrance when on the platform, are secondary when people are rubbing shoulders.

The second method to unlock the involvement of the community is a survey of the resources of the area, material and human, preferably conducted by some of the residents themselves. This should identify the material resources that are going to waste, notably derelict or under-used buildings, but as well the human skills that are under- or unemployed. It should identify the more positive aspects of the area — perhaps its community spirit, a beautiful building, the surrounding countryside or a country walk — the things people enjoy. The result will record, probably for the first time, the frequently hidden resources of the community and the place in which it lives.

The ideas and possibilities revealed by the model and the latent resources revealed by the survey can then be drawn together in a feasibility study, the one helping to meet the needs of the other. By this stage, even if it did not initiate the process, one or more of the local authorities is virtually certain to be involved in some form. They should be able to find ways in which the findings of the study can be assisted towards reality, by small grants or loans, which on a multiplier basis can lead to bigger sums, by the availability of items of equipment or transport and technical advice. Both the local community and the authorities should respond positively to the ingenuity implicit in carrying out projects on a shoestring, but once the objectives are clear, the resources quantified and preferably initial work on a project is under way, the extra funding that is likely to be required can be sought from the financial institutions. The partnership that has been established between the official organisations and the community, including its voluntary groups, may appeal to their imagination, the more so if it is supported by professional advice, evidence of the anticipated incremental growth of several small initiatives and the goodwill of the community.

The technique is only applicable to small communities, although there is no reason why they should not be part of larger ones, because it is inherent that everyone who wishes to can be involved and that results should be achieved quickly.

To co-ordinate this many-sided and ambitious objective, the organisation managing the project needs the services of a highly motivated team leader or manager, who is used to meeting people, experienced in the range of economic, social, planning and architectural issues that will arise in the course of the project and is familiar with the working of local organisations and the various funding agencies. The project leader must be aware of his or her limitations, be able to identify the fields in which more expertise is needed and have the authority to obtain the support of specialists as necessary. He or she will require premises in the place concerned from which to provide information, answer questions from members of the public and in which small gatherings of people can meet. Administrative support will be required.

The pump-priming required is partly of cash, but equally important it is of ideas and enthusiasm. The variety of people actively contributing to the work of the buildings preservation trusts proves that this can be found in all walks of life. Particularly if an independent, outside body can prepare the ground, it is possible that a local organisation, a different one in different places, may be equipped to take a leading role or that one of the local authorities, seeing the benefits that would accrue, has the right staff for the task. The early steps in the Wirksworth project were all taken by an influential, independent charitable organisation which not only conceived the idea but obtained the help of another charity to provide the funds. Being independent and unencumbered by previous local involvement, it was well placed to make a fresh start on building up the trust, goodwill and confidence of the community. Local organisations, the town and county councils, later took over.

This is a formula that could be adopted and adapted in other places. The reviving of a whole community requires an alliance of interests much more than a single repair project. Within this alliance, individual renovation schemes, promoted officially or voluntarily, can make a vital contribution.

171

14
TECHNICAL

Professional assistance

For any project to be successful it is necessary to be able to call on a range of professional skills and to weld them into a project team. The expertise that will be needed may vary slightly from one scheme to the next. Grants may be available for fees. The following are likely to be needed at one stage or another or throughout:

Architect   For initial survey work, feasibility, outline design proposals, detailed plans, obtaining local authority approvals, advice on engaging a building contractor and supervision. The RIBA conditions of appointment provide for partial services. The early work is usually the most critical.

Quantity Surveyor   For feasibility costings and cost advice and control. This advice is particularly helpful in larger projects.

Accountant   Voluntary bodies may need an accountant to prepare cash-flow projections when making grant or loan applications, to prepare an annual statement of accounts, advise on tax matters and generally keep an eye on the finances.

Solicitor   For advice on the constitution and charitable status of a voluntary body and contractual matters and obligations. Some solicitors also specialise in tax and insurance matters.

Clerk of Works   Large or complex projects may require supervision by a clerk of works who can be appointed to see that the provisions of the contract are properly carried out. Normally, a clerk of works is employed full-time but it may be appropriate to make a part-time appointment.

Estate Agents   For advice on market values and marketing. Estate agents tend to specialise in certain types of properties and locations. The appointed agent or agents should be enthusiastic about the aims of the scheme. If a single agent is appointed for sales purposes it may be sensible to limit the period of appointment so that progress can be reviewed and additional agents brought in if necessary.

172

Depending on the needs of the scheme, specialist advice may also be required on detailed aspects from a structural, mechanical, electrical or civil engineer, a landscape architect and perhaps on town planning matters. For any given scheme the architect will be able to advise on the range of expertise that is likely to be necessary for the building work.

SELECTING AN ARCHITECT

The architect needs to be well versed in the techniques of renovation, knowledgeable about the historical styles of buildings and possess an imaginative flair that will produce solutions in ostensibly unpromising situations. A large local authority, such as a county council, may well possess people of suitable calibre, in which case they can be appointed if available. Smaller authorities are more likely to need to seek either county council or private practice help. A voluntary organisation could approach a local authority department for advice or assistance, but it is more usual to appoint an architect in private practice. Whichever organisation is carrying out the project, the right architect may not be immediately obvious and to help in such cases the RIBA has a client advisory service that will provide a list of suitable architects in practice in the area concerned (Client Advisory Service, RIBA, 66 Portland Place, London W1N 4AD).

Using the list, which might equally be compiled on the basis of adequate personal knowledge, relevant practices and schemes architects have carried out can be visited without prejudice to the final appointment. On this basis, a shortlist of architects can be invited to discuss the project. The final choice should rest solely on the architect's suitability for the project. A little trouble in making a good appointment will be repaid as the project takes shape.

In the case of local authority-run schemes, the authority may itself be equipped to carry out initial survey or feasibility work, even where detailed later stages are to be handled by consultants. In such cases, the consultants' terms of appointment should allow full scope for the beneficial use of his/their own ideas and advice.

The quantity surveyor, particularly in larger projects, is also a key member of the building team. As with the architect, he should be experienced in renovation work. Some firms of architects encompass quantity surveying work. It is sensible to obtain the project architect's advice concerning the appointment as both the architect and the quantity surveyor will need to work together and must have confidence in each other.

A close working relationship should quickly be established between

173

the management side of the voluntary organisation or the local authority carrying out the project and its chief technical advisers.

Although price is a crucial factor in selecting a builder, it is not the only factor. It is also important that he should be reliable, have a sympathetic attitude towards the type of work proposed and be able to call on the trade skills that are required. The architect will be able to advise on a list of such builders, but a local authority will first have to advertise the contract and draw up a list from the replies received. Depending on the size of the job it can often be useful to invite the builders that appear most suitable to discuss the work proposed. This can be of help to them and to the organisation proposing the scheme, particularly where the work is of a complex nature.

The kind of information that may be revealed by interviews with builders before tender stage is illustrated in the following exchanges which took place prior to the letting of the contract for the first phase of Suffolk Coastal District Council's scheme in New Street, Woodbridge. The interviews are recorded by kind permission of the council and its consultant architects, Messrs Feilden & Mawson, and are two out of seven that were held.

Builder 1

A (Architect) What are your views on the site as far as conservation is concerned?

B (Builder) I have strong views on conservation. I feel that renovation and conservation is in preference to pulling down buildings. I live at Ufford, 2 miles away, and I know Woodbridge well.

A No 63 will be demolished to allow for access. However, there will be a problem of scaffolding when working on No 55 as the pavement is narrow.

B We would visit the site to ascertain the difficulties involved when pricing.

A [Explanation of first of one or two phases. Also explanation of problem of overlap of No 53 with 55 and care that must be taken not to damage No 53.] It will be essential to replace existing materials with the same type of material. Do you have access to second-hand materials?

B Yes, we have an associate company which gives us access to second-hand materials.

A The bricks from No 63 will only be used for patching. When new

174

walls are built, new bricks will be billed for but if you have access to suitable second-hand bricks these will be considered.

You have thirty employees. Obviously you have several contracts going at one time. What would you suggest would be the approximate number of men to be used on this site?

B About six men.

A If you found you were running late on the contract period, would you call on other men?

B Yes, but we usually like to keep within the contract time.

A What would you say would be the approximate contract period required?

B I never like to guess on this sort of thing. It will probably be about twenty-four weeks but I shall be able to be more precise when I have seen the Bill of Quantities.

A We are aiming at sectional completion and the handing over of one unit at a time from No 55 upwards.

B This will be all right but it depends what sort of time difference you mean. I would move on from one property to another with only the final finishes to be done.

A We shall be billing the services on the Bill of Quantities so that the contractor will either quote for them or sub-contract.

B This will suit us well. We have associate companies in other trades.

A Do you have your own joinery shop?

B Yes.

A We ask this because we need to be sure that the contractor can supply the specialist fitments we ask for and not supplement with what he thinks.

B I agree with this. We have done restoration work in the London area and worked on Regency terraces. We have two joiners and a boy in the shop and we hope to have just enough to do what is needed.

A Would a fixed-price contract be acceptable?

B Yes.

A [Explanation of itemising in the bill to help identification.]

B I am pleased that Suffolk Coastal are preparing bills for this job as in the past there has been a tendency not to do so. What will you be doing with the top floor?

A This will be purely storage space and the gas boiler will be installed there.

175

Builder 2
A This is a conservation job. Have you done much of this type of work?
B I have done very little conservation work.
A Have you looked at the site?
B When I first looked at the site I was amazed anybody was bothering with them. What are you going to do with the attics?
A These will remain as storage spaces and the water tanks and gas boilers will be installed there.
   [Explanation of importance of conservation area work and the two sewer connections to be made to the road.]
B Can I use the bricks from No 63 on the other properties?
A Yes, some of them but there will not be enough and you will have to find more. You have five employees. Will all these be allocated to this one job?
B I only take one job on at a time and finish one job before taking on another. I am trying to keep my staff down at the moment.
A There will be a contract period. What would you do if you found you could not adhere to this period?
B I would take on extra staff. I dislike using existing materials. In some cases it is not possible to repair existing fitments, etc.
A We shall be going into such details more deeply. However, the sort of things that are asked for should be provided.
B I have the facilities to get the parts.
A As you will have to find sub-contractors, would you rather extend your tender period from twenty-one days?
B Yes, I might need five weeks.
A Does the six months contract period still stand?
B No. A lot of work will have to be done on the building before individual cottages are worked on. Six months will not be long enough — I would think about eight or nine months.
A What type of contract would you prefer?
B I have never worked with local authorities, but I normally work on a fixed-price contract.
A Do you hire any plant or scaffolding?
B I have a lot of my own plant and scaffolding but I probably have not got enough at the moment for this job. Is the wall next to No 63 included in the demolition work?
A Yes.
B What will you do with the site of demolition afterwards?
A We have to supply parking areas and we hope to provide a small garden for No 61.

B   The only thing I am worried about is the drains. Are they very far
     down in the road?
A   We believe they are only about 2ft down and therefore will have to
     be hand dug.

Builder 1 was invited to tender and was successful in obtaining the contract. Builder 2 was not invited to tender.

Should specialist skills be required, a register of craftsmen and
specialist workshops is kept by the Crafts Council, 12 Waterloo Place,
London SW1Y 4AN, and which may be consulted locally at county and
district planning departments.

Statutory requirements
PLANNING PERMISSION

The responsibility for planning at a local level rests with the district
council, from which advice should be sought at an early stage.
Although any proposed development which involves changes in use of
buildings or any new building or extension to existing buildings generally requires planning permission, there are a number of exceptions,
which are set out in the General Development Order.

The planning authority will welcome the opportunity to discuss
proposals informally before an application is submitted and will provide details of what information the application should contain.
Depending on the complexity of the work proposed and whether or not
change of use only is required, applications can either be for outline or
full permission. Outline applications in respect of listed buildings are
often discouraged.

Most applications containing proposals of substance are considered
by local councillors at committee where they are advised by the planning
officer. If the local committee member can be advised of the proposals
and fully briefed before they reach the committee stage, it can often be
helpful. The council must consider the proposal in the light of its general
planning policies and its effect on the area and the amenities of any local
residents. In some areas, such as National Parks or Areas of Outstanding Natural Beauty (AONB), there may be special requirements. The
local authority will provide information about these.

If an application is refused or unacceptable conditions are imposed,
an appeal can be made to the DoE. Unless a proposal raises issues of
considerable public interest, when a local enquiry may be held, an
appeal is likely to be dealt with by written representations. But, because
of the delay and uncertainty involved, it is normally better to avoid the

appeal process by agreeing a mutually acceptable basis for the application with the planning officer at the outset. In most cases such a basis will be acceptable to the committee, but it should be remembered that the committee has the right to have the final say. The period from the submission of the application to the decision by the committee is normally two months.

LISTED BUILDING CONSENT AND REPAIRS NOTICES

Each local authority has lists of buildings in its area that are classified by the DoE as being of special architectural or historic interest. According to their importance, there are three grades of listed buildings, Grade I, Grade II star and Grade II. These buildings cannot be demolished or altered in any way which affects their character unless listed building consent has been obtained from the local planning authority. Listed building consent must also be obtained for the demolition of unlisted buildings in conservation areas.

The interpretation of 'character' is crucial to listed building consent and should be discussed with the local planning or conservation officer. Generally, repair works are not held to need consent but restoration work can, if it involves, for example, the reinstatement of a feature of the building that did not exist when it was listed, even if it can be shown that it was part of the original design.

The statutory responsibility for the preservation of a listed building rests with the owner. Failure to meet this responsibility can entitle the local authority to serve on the owner a repairs notice which lists the items of work that are needed to put the structure in good repair. Failure to comply with the notice can lead to compulsory purchase by the authority, subject to the Secretary of State for the Environment's final sanction. Some local authorities are reluctant to use the repairs notice power because it can finish up by acquiring and assuming direct responsibility for a building in poor condition for which it has no use or resources to renovate. However, if a ready buyer is available, in the shape of a private purchaser, a voluntary group such as a buildings preservation trust or even a council's in-house revolving fund, the risk need be only minimal. Largely because of the existence of the buildings preservation trust in the wings to purchase if necessary, Hampshire County Council has made effective use of the repairs notice procedure, without the need for further action by the trust. The 1981 annual report of the Hampshire Buildings Preservation Trust noted that, 'Whilst it has supported some 20 Repairs Notices, for example, it has not so far been necessary for the Trust to intervene, as none has led to compulsory purchase by the local authority. Offers to purchase by agreement have, similarly, often resulted in sale to another owner.'

BUILDING REGULATIONS

Building regulations are concerned with the technical standards of construction of buildings and their basic fittings, and cover new and alteration work. Plans and sometimes calculations need to be submitted to the local authority building surveyor, or to the district surveyor in the case of the London boroughs.

The regulations set out minimum standards and are complicated. If they are applied unsympathetically they can have a devastating effect on historic buildings in regard, for example, to room heights, window openings and staircases and balustrades. To avoid this, it may be necessary to apply for a relaxation of the regulations, but generally — and particularly if they are involved at an early stage — local authority officials will do their best to overcome conflict with the requirements of historic buildings, as was illustrated in the Collin Croft project in Kendal. The local officials who help to find a sensible path through the rules and regulations play an essential, and largely unsung, part in the renovation process.

FIRE REGULATIONS

Fire precautions normally come under building regulations but if specialised advice is required the Fire Authority (county council) should be contacted. The means of escape and fire-fighting equipment must meet specified standards in public buildings and in shops and offices, and approval will be needed from the Fire Authority. The local authority building surveyor will advise initially.

HEALTH REGULATIONS

Refuse disposal, noise emission and pollution, standards covering premises where food and drink is served and the adequate provision of toilet facilities in public buildings are among the responsibilities of the local authority's Environmental Health Department. Refuse disposal in particular should be considered at an early stage, as the standards that the local authority stipulate can sometimes have a substantial effect on the design and layout of a project.

STATUTORY UNDERTAKERS

Gas, water and electricity supplies must be installed in accordance with the relevant authorities' regulations.

All public buildings must allow reasonable access to and provision for the disabled. The local authority will provide detailed information.

Freehold and leasehold sales

A freehold is a property held free of duty for an indefinite period, whereas a leasehold involves the regular payment of a sum of money to the freeholder for a specified period. Most residential property is freehold but flats and maisonettes are normally sold leasehold because they involve the multi-occupation of a single property and the need to secure the maintenance, by means of rent, of communal areas. Commercial properties are also normally sold on a leasehold basis. So a scheme consisting of shops on the ground floor with self-contained residential accommodation above will be sold leasehold.

Unless a developer is able to dispose of the freehold of such a scheme to a third party, he will assume the responsibility of making arrangements for the management of the property, collecting rents, carrying out any repairs that are not the responsibility of the leaseholder, and generally seeing that the terms of the individual leases are complied with. While none of this presents difficulties to a local authority, a small trust may feel that this essentially management role is not their function. Where this problem has occurred, trusts have therefore set up separate management companies to administer the leases, as in the Bradford-on-Avon Preservation Trust's scheme for the conversion into flats of a large house in Silver Street.

It may be possible to sell the freehold, perhaps to a small local investment trust or to an investor looking primarily for a steady, long-term income. To do this, the income represented by the freehold needs to be attractive to the investor and, as the income is set out in the terms of the lease, the decision to sell or retain the freehold needs to be taken before those terms are finalised. A balance needs to be struck between the capital and rental elements in the value of the scheme: the greater the amount of capital received for the leases, the less the amount of rent that can be charged, and vice versa. The advice of a valuer or of a solicitor or surveyor experienced in estate management is essential.

The straightforward sale of the freehold, as in most house sales, is the simplest way of keeping capital turning over, but the additional arrangements that are necessary for leasehold properties should not discourage the introduction of uses requiring a lease when the demand in the location concerned is for those uses. Housing for rent, rather than sale, has been the stock-in-trade of the Amsterdam Company for Town Restoration since 1956, and in city-centre locations flats and mixed uses, requiring leases, will often be what is required by the market. The Company provides houses and flats for rent and in effect combines the virtues of a housing authority, a housing association and a buildings preservation trust. It uses the rental income to pay off interest on its loans and to pay dividends to its shareholders. It now possesses about 300 properties in Amsterdam's inner city, and a staff of seventeen, including eight in a building department, are required to manage them.

Market value, marketing and mortgages

Since the raw material of buildings preservation trust work and of local authority revolving funds often stands in streets or places that have for long been run-down and unfashionable, a newly renovated building may well, in these surroundings, shine like a beacon until the improving habit takes hold and spreads. Value will not be easy to assess, because comparable properties in comparable situations may not exist and property values may only settle down to a more easily predictable level in a year or two when neighbouring properties may also have been improved. But the vendor almost certainly cannot wait that long. To achieve an early return of capital, asking prices will need to be decided sooner rather than later.

Local authorities will be advised by the district valuer or their own valuation staff; trusts may seek the advice of estate agents. Either way, some thought should be given to the market and the local factors that might influence or be influenced by the type of purchaser envisaged and the values in the scheme — in Suffolk the locally depressed values in New Street were increased by the scheme to general Woodbridge levels but, because of external economic factors, the Leiston scheme appears to have had no effect on prevailing values. Much of this will have been considered at the earlier, feasibility stage, when an estate agent's opinion may be useful, but assessments of this sort early on are especially difficult. They can be upset by longer term movements in the economy as well as by local factors, and it may not be easy to convey to the agent concerned the full effect of the alteration work envisaged and he is likely to take a cautious view. More than one opinion, early on or when the time comes to place the properties on the market, may be helpful together with a certain amount of homework.

Estate agents tend to specialise in certain types of property. Familiarity with and interest in the type of scheme concerned and support for its objectives should translate into imaginative and effective marketing.

181

The agent should be on the look-out for purchasers seeking something a little out of the ordinary, even those who may have in mind spending much more for a house of character and quality than is being asked for the project, the value of which may be depressed by its location. The appointment of an agent can be discussed with perhaps three or four firms in order to assess their attitudes and experience. A sole agent will normally offer more competitive terms and have a greater incentive to market the scheme successfully than a shared appointment, but any sole agency should be for a limited period only to enable additional agents to be appointed if necessary.

As soon as a scheme is completed and a valuer can see the final product, some building societies will value the individual properties and agree, hopefully, on a similar basis to the vendor's estimates, the range of prices on which they would make offers of mortgage. This may be done before completion, particularly if the scheme is straightforward. A bank may also agree to this approach, depending on how keen it is to be involved in the mortgage market. In order to encourage agreement on a mortgage facility at the earliest possible stage, reference to the agreement could be included on the sale signboard which, if it is in a prominent position, might be an attractive advertisement for the building society or bank concerned. The vendor cannot, of course, insist on a purchaser using the mortgage facility, but the more it is publicised the better, and if a purchaser's own mortgagee comes up with a capriciously low offer an alternative is available. Because of the lack of comparison and the difficulties of achieving a generally agreed valuation, individual valuers, acting for a building society or a bank, may fall back on highly personal assessments. In the Leiston project there were wide discrepancies, amounting to about 25 per cent, in offers made on the same property. This can be upsetting to both purchaser and vendor and can result in sales falling through, particularly if there is no alternative to hand.

Publicity and sales promotion overlap. Sufficient general publicity may reduce, or even avoid, the need for particular sales promotion. An informative signboard should be erected on site, perhaps including an illustration of the scheme when completed. At significant stages of the work — the start of or the completion of a phase of building work, interesting architectural or archaeological finds, the removal of the scaffolding, the first property completed, sold or occupied — the local press, which will probably follow progress closely, should be informed. Formal opening and exhibitions on the Suffolk pattern should result in good publicity and may be of interest to television. All this will reflect well on the project's sponsors, council or trust. It may also produce purchasers.

After-sales service and alterations
On 26 April 1981, a purchaser of a renovated house in New Street, Woodbridge, Suffolk wrote to Suffolk Coastal District Council: 'As a result of the recent high winds and heavy rain on April 24th, 25th and 26th, water is once again dripping through the ceiling.' At times of strong south-westerly winds, seepage of rainwater through the roof had been an intermittent and puzzling problem in this property from the time the purchaser had moved in early in 1980. Previous attempts to identify the cause had been unsuccessful. Following the purchaser's complaint in April 1981, the contractor was asked to remove the old pantiles from the section of roof concerned and a tear was found in the felt underlay, an essential second-line of defence against water percolation with roof coverings of this sort in particularly adverse weather conditions. After the felt had been replaced there was no further problem. The contractor accepted full responsibility.

Purchasers who have invested a substantial part of their savings in a restored property or have the burden of monthly repayments on a mortgage or bank loan will expect their property to function in a proper and convenient manner. If defects occur soon after occupation, they should be investigated without delay in order to identify the cause and to apportion responsibility. At the same time, purchasers should be aware that the properties, being old, should not be expected to comply with full modern standards and that the responsibility for maintenance is theirs.

The dividing line between defects and maintenance can be a difficult one to draw. The leaking roof was clearly a defect. It had shown up soon after occupation, the council had been notified immediately and no other party had been involved. The cause was faulty workmanship by the contractor, which he readily accepted, but it is not always so clear-cut. A television aerial contractor employed by the purchaser could inadvertently dislodge a roof slate or a tile and the damage might be undetected for several weeks until revealed by high winds. Minor plaster shrinkage cracks are likely to occur for some time after occupation, particularly in areas of new work and where central heating is installed. Some purchasers or their agents will expect higher or different standards from others. The use of existing or second-hand materials may well be an essential element in the historic appeal of a scheme, but it may not prevent their use being criticised by an agent making a report on behalf of a prospective purchaser. To try to forestall criticisms of this type and to assist the new owners with their maintenance responsibilities, it may be appropriate to provide purchasers with a maintenance manual or a few sheets of notes providing information on the properties, as was done in the Derby Railway Cottages and the Leiston High Green projects. Suitable advice can avoid expensive problems in the future.

Normally the terms of a builder's contract provide for a six-month period of maintenance by the contractor after the building work is completed. Timber treatment and damp proofing should be covered by long-term guarantees given by specialist firms of sub-contractors. In addition, there is general common law protection against faulty workmanship for a period of six years from the completion of the work.

Trusts are required, as part of their articles, to include whatever covenants are necessary to ensure that the character and historic interest of the property concerned is preserved on a permanent basis, and local authorities may also wish to include suitable covenants in their sales contracts. Even in the case of listed buildings, owners may alter external paint colours or add garden sheds without permission, unless provision is made in the contract for the consent of the vendor to be obtained. The importance of alterations or additions of this sort will vary from project to project. The Derby Railway Cottages were all painted externally in the crimson lake and cream colours of the Midland Railway Company which built them originally, and in this case it was important that the purchasers should be required to keep to the colour scheme. Terraced properties generally look best with a co-ordinated scheme of colours. The appearance of a large property could be ruined if individual owners had a free hand when repainting. Even garden sheds could spoil the outlook for neighbours in the case of urban properties with tiny backyards, and the gradual accumulation of a number of even individually minor items can harm the appearance and unity of a group of buildings. Whilst too many restrictions are unreasonable, and probably unworkable, if a building has exceptional quality a firm approach is justified. Covenants can be included to control items such as verandahs or conservatories that might have been excluded from the builder's contract to reduce costs, perhaps with the needs of first-time buyers in mind. Minor additions such as these can sensibly be left to purchasers as and when they can afford them, but only as long as there is adequate control over their design. Wherever possible, it is best to include such items at the outset. A balance needs to be struck that takes account of all the circumstances of the scheme.

15

VOLUNTARY GROUPS AS AGENCIES

The overhead costs of voluntary groups tend to be significantly lower than those of larger organisations, official or commercial, doing similar work. Normally, they have no permanent premises to pay for and to heat and light. Their office may be a table in their honorary secretary's living-room or a tidied-up and reasonably weathertight corner of a current scheme. Wages are often nominal and the cost of the capital employed is reduced by public fund raising, and low- or no-interest loans. Charities are eligible for rate relief, in part or whole, on properties owned by them. Because of this, the overheads element in the cost of a project carried out by a voluntary organisation is likely to be comparatively low. This should enable them to carry out projects exceptionally economically and permit less promising schemes to be undertaken.

This advantage affects all building types and uses, but in some cases — as with the provision of low-rent accommodation for small-starter businesses — the reduction of project costs, leading to lower rental costs, can be crucial. Many local authorities, wishing to attract jobs to their areas, could look to a buildings preservation trust to carry out, for example, the purchase and conversion of a Victorian warehouse or maltings so as to exploit the trust's capacity to minimise administrative costs and obtain cheap capital, and then by prior agreement, purchase from the trust the finished scheme at cost. The authority would pass on the savings to the leaseholders who, in turn, would have the rental element in their own costs reduced, so making their businesses more viable. For its part, the trust would have the satisfaction of carrying out a scheme of importance to the community and of conservation value to the town or district. On completion it would have the certainty of a purchaser.

The principle of the voluntary group as an agency can be applied in other fields such as housing, public buildings and office accommodation. It seems a natural progression in their development as organisations solely concerned with projects of benefit to the community.

16

LOCAL AUTHORITY REVOLVING FUNDS AS AGENCIES

Although it lacks the appeal of the voluntary group's low overheads, a local authority which operates its own revolving fund can use this as an agency to provide accommodation in run-down buildings and areas. If a scheme has important job creation or social benefits as well as a heritage conservation aspect, there is a good case for even a loss-making project, supported on the revolving principle by gains on schemes elsewhere. To do this effectively, every opportunity needs to be taken in the management of the revolving fund to carry out as many profitable schemes as possible, even in competition with private, commercial organisations, for the larger the surplus on these the greater is the scope for unviable projects. It implies an aggressive, entrepreneurial style of revolving-fund management, actively seeking schemes rather than passively waiting only for those that no other organisation will accept.

POSTSCRIPT

Patrick Nuttgens

To anyone reviewing today's environment, the most obvious and inescapable fact is change. Since the mid-fifties, when the stringent controls of the immediate post-war years were relaxed, we have been indulging in an orgy of urban change — little less than the transformation of our towns and cities. It has affected every physical aspect of their life — housing, offices, public buildings, traffic. In particular it involved what in my student days was regarded as one of the great discoveries and objectives of modern planning — comprehensive redevelopment.

The change was not only in the towns. Changes in the countryside are not quite so obtrusive to the ordinary observer, but in the last few decades they have been every bit as fundamental. Most of the rural landscape of this country is man-made, the long-term result of the agricultural revolution of the seventeenth and eighteenth centuries, which gave us our present field systems, the crops and animals, the hedges and walls and more obvious features of arcadian England. In the last thirty years we have been witnessing just as profound an agricultural revolution, with dramatic changes in productivity, in land utilisation, in rural population and in rural building: 90 per cent of farm buildings, I am told, are strictly speaking redundant, the patterns of cultivation of the land change annually, hedges are torn up and field boundaries disappear. So do people. The countryside is now more deserted than at any previous period in history.

We have in short experienced the most massive and comprehensive environmental changes. Such changes are often gradual and sometimes seem trivial. But small features in the end affect the character of the whole. And that change is something best described, not as a set of statistics, but as a change in the grain of town and country, something more profound than appearances, a change and movement in their underlying structure and social fabric.

One of the results — probably the inevitable result sooner or later of such drastic changes — is protest. It's not only local or even national; it's international; it's everywhere. Anyone engaged in the practice of planning and design knows that they will not put forward any serious planning scheme at present that is not met by a storm of protest. I suspect that in Britain at the moment — not only in the environment but also in one or two other areas of work with which I am involved, such as education — no change would actually be the best possible thing. But it ought, I believe, to be for the right reason; and I doubt if the right reason is fear of change and fear of the future. As an old country slowly adjusting itself to a minor role in the affairs of the world, we suffer from that fear. But we also have in front of our eyes in the physical scene some reason for the belief that inspires many of our protests and amenity movements — that the future will be worse than the past.

That is the negative aspect of conservation and it nearly always gets things started. But conservation has now taken on another dimension. The concept of the architectural heritage has been getting wider in the last few years. It used to consist of major buildings — cathedrals, country houses, great commercial and public buildings; it was then widened to include many building types that a few years ago would have failed to qualify — factories, housing, schools, universities and colleges, and many types of social and industrial building — bridges, canals, railways, even roads, all the technological impedimenta of an urban society. And, of course, landscape. The Town and Country Amenities Act of 1974 included 'historic landscapes' in its provisions.

In effect, what this means is that what was once regarded as the 'architectural heritage' now involves the study of the whole environment. The seminal buildings of now and the near future are likely to be not so much the isolated works of idiosyncratic genius as those which are generated by a concern for the total environment and the fusion of buildings and landscape. If that is so, it follows that the major design movement of our time should be conservation — of nature as well as of resources, facilities, land and buildings. And that means their preservation and enhancement for the benefit of the community.

Some of the documents published on the subject by the Council of Europe a few years ago emphasised how wide is the scope of the movement. They pointed out that 'the architectural heritage is no longer looked upon simply as a set of monuments of aesthetic value but as the expression of the cultural, social and economic interests of the community which produced it and imbued it with life'. They stress the concept of the 'human environment' and the need for a comprehensive approach. For we are concerned with the 'quality of life' and thus with the utilisation and re-utilisation of the heritage as part of a comprehensive regional planning policy. To do that we must explore contemporary planning problems in the context of people and history. For the socio-historical context is vital to an understanding of problems 'with reference to the evolution of European society and its effects upon land utilisation'.

There are several important concepts here which reflect the way in which the subject is treated and the shift in emphasis which has occurred. If the architectural heritage is essentially the expression of the cultural, social and economic interests of the community, it is clear that we are concerned not just with physical objects, whatever their value, but with a socio-economic and cultural phenomenon. That has ultimately to do with Man; it is a human environment, not just a physical one. It follows that conserving the heritage — the concept of conservation — is not, in the eyes of its promoters, a happy attempt to cheer up the environment and improve its looks; it is an activity profoundly affecting the evolution of society. The medium for its implementation is the utilisation and re-utilisation of the heritage — new uses for old places. That exercise lies close to the very heart of civilisation; for, as Lethaby said, 'the civic arts are the arts of civilisation and the arts of civilisation are civilisation itself'.

In terms of the practical activity of doing something about the heritage, conservation means in the words of the Civic Trust, 'integrated conservation'. That is to say, it must involve all building types, both buildings and land, all social classes and social groups; it must involve both life and work, both use and appearance. And the phrase which has been happily coined to denote the way in which conservation can flourish is

"This is Mr Trimp from the Town and Country Planning Department. He's here to demonstrate the proposals for the old town"

'creative continuity' — the continuity of the total human environment in the midst of change.

There have been periods in history, such as the eighteenth century, when the landscape — and indeed the total environment — could be seen as a reflection of the search by artists and writers for order and unity. We, however, are a pragmatic, self-centred, materialistic society, concerned with people and places and rather less with concepts and systems of thought. We have no great unifying idea in a pluralistic society, though I am sure we feel a need for a place in continuity. We need roots, to belong somewhere and in some time.

It is made more urgent by the very characteristics of our society — the child of the Industrial Revolution, of constant technological change, of the electronic revolution, of continuing revolutions in fuels. We have witnessed the uprooting of communities on a scale which the barbarisms of history did not contrive; we are mobile; we have access to more information and education than ever before. And yet, we need to belong somewhere, to be part of some system. Among the great popular social movements of our time are not movements away from it all — that is a minority and privileged attitude — but into it all, if necessary into a vast totalitarian bureaucracy. How much more humane, more personal, more free, to have a place, not in such a system, but in time — in continuity! The significant change in the thinking, the ideas, of our time may be a move away from a concept of unity as a static hierarchy, towards a unity in time, sequential, changing and ever moving, subject to laws, not of order and permanence, but of flow and change and growth and decay.

In that situation, fundamental to any kind of conservation is the use of old buildings. That means their study, ordering and sometimes modification for contemporary needs. It is the prerequisite for their survival; we cannot make use of any number of museums. In the same way, the essence of integrated conservation is the use of old landcapes, which effectively means all land. That involves an understanding of how it can be used, not just of its financial value.

Any meaningful unity of the environment must depend ultimately upon use, upon the daily life of the place, and that means upon the unity of its functions, its needs and its visual feaures. Use and appearance are always linked; it is the correspondence of the two, one being an expression of the other, that ultimately creates an architecture or an environment which is both aesthetically satisfying and practically sound. The ultimate design task for a conservationist is to use all the bits of the heritage that must be kept, to select what other bits seem significant, to make additions and weld it all into a new unity which will be valid for the community he serves.

In such a process of conservation and creativity, the study and conclusions reached in Michael Talbot's book are of both immediate and lasting importance. It is even characteristic of the movement that it should start in Scotland with Little Houses rather than in England with Great Houses. And it is of the very nature of the continuity of the environment that it should embrace the concept of 'revolving conservation', using the profits as well as the experience of one project to initiate and finance the next. Ultimately the country has to survive as what it is already — an endless exercise in creative continuity.

I have tried in this postscript to identify conservation as a phase in the rediscovery of a more basic idea of continuity. I believe that the idea of continuity is not just a superficial label to be attached to a passing phase of design or aesthetics; it is a philosophical concept capable of informing a big part of our lives. As such it has immediate significance for us in a pluralistic society without much confidence about the future or much trace of that optimism which characterised the eighteenth century. It is a recognition of our temporality and transience; it is also a recognition of our sense of isolation and powerlessness in the complexity of a technological urban civilisation and culture.

With everything I read and explore, I become more convinced that any attempt to live and work consciously in a context of continuity can only be good. I am convinced that our environment, like our lives, has already partly disintegrated and that that disintegration is serious. In the words of a writer in the *Architects Journal*, it 'testifies with an unbearable honesty to our social and spiritual disintegration'. A demand to bring it together again, to create out of it a new unity, is not a sentimental protest; it is a statement of social and personal needs.

Appendix I
GRANT-MAKING TRUSTS

The following is a list of trusts specialising in, or including amongst projects aided, historic buildings and environmental improvement and education. *Indicates local area of interest.

The Baring Foundation*
The Secretary, 8 Bishopgate, London EC2N 4AE
For projects in London or of major national significance.

J. & L. A. Cadbury Charitable Trust
The Secretary, 2 College Walk, Birmingham B29 6LE
National and local projects outside London.

Laura Capel Charitable Trust
MacFarlanes, Dowgate Hill House, London EC4R 2SY
Supports registered charities only.

The Carnegie United Kingdom Trust
The Secretary, 80 New Row, Dunfermline, Fife KY12 7EJ
The trust has a particular interest in co-operation between voluntary and statutory bodies and in environmental interpretation, including heritage centres. Its annual report is lodged in public and university libraries. Enquiries at an early stage in project planning are welcomed.

The Wilfred and Constance Cave Foundation*
Everleigh, Marlborough, Wiltshire
Donates only to local charities or ones with which the trustees are personally acquainted, chiefly in Wiltshire. No postal applications considered.

The Chase Society
General Secretary, 10 Barley Mow Passage, Chiswick, London W4 4PH
Concentrates on small organisations in the UK, including starter finance and unforeseen expenditure outside normal budgets.

D. C. W. Trust
The Secretary, 129 Battenhall Road, Worcester
Supports registered charities only.

Mr James A. De Rothschild's Charitable Settlement
Messrs Saffery, Sons & Co, St Martin's House, 16 St Martin's-le-Grand, London EC1A 4EP

This trust covers a broad field and historic buildings account for a relatively small part of its interest.

Esmee Fairbairn Trust Fund
The Director, 10 Fleet Street, London EC4Y 1AN
The preservation of the heritage is widely supported, most particularly enterprising projects. Beneficiaries must be registered charities.

Lord Faringdon Charitable Trust
C/o William Sturgis, Trotter & Co, 55 The Mall, Ealing, London W5 3TB
Particular interest in museums.

Four Winds Trust
64 Ravenscourt Gardens, Ravenscourt Park, London W6 0TH
Projects related to the countryside by registered charities.

The Granada Foundation*
Granada Television Centre, Manchester M60 9EA
Concentrates on projects in the north west of England involving education or leisure facilities and producing benefits to a wide public.

The Gresham Charitable Trust
Brebner, Allen & Trapp, 109 Baker Street, London W1M 2BH
Recurrent operational expenses or specific projects involving capital expenditure by registered charities are assisted over a very wide field, of which building conservation is only a part.

The Grimley Charity*
Messrs Ryland Martineau & Co, 41 Church Street, Birmingham B3 2DY
The trust supports mainly Worcestershire charities.

Grocers Charity
Grocers Hall, Princes Street, London EC2R 8AQ
Assists registered charities only, preferably national, over a wide field.

The Hambland Foundation
The Secretary, 10 Barley Mow Passage, Chiswick, London W4 4PH
Grants are normally on a once-only basis and are made to registered charities only.

The Hawthorne Charitable Trust
Messrs Howard, Tilly & Co, Commonwealth House, 1 New Oxford Street, London WC1A 1PF
Makes grants for general charitable purposes.

Hickinbotham Charitable Trust*
69 Main Street, Busby, Leicestershire LE7 9PL
For charitable trust work in Leicestershire.

Kleinwort Benson Charitable Trust
Kleinwort Benson Ltd, 20 Fenchurch Street, London EC3P 3DB
Responds to national appeals only from registered charities.

The Sir Cyril Kleinwort Charitable Settlement*
The Secretary, Trustee Department, Kleinwort Benson Ltd, 20 Fenchurch
Street, London EC3P 3DB
*Most of the trust's income is committed to the continuing support of charities already known
to them. Projects should be of a national standing or of particular interest to the county of
Gloucestershire.*

The Ernest Kleinwort Charitable Trust*
The Secretary, Kleinwort Benson Ltd, 20 Fenchurch Street, London EC3P 3DB
*The trust supports national charities and local charities in Sussex, managed by persons of
proven business ability. It specialises in short-period loans to launch specific projects.*

The Langtree Trust*
Fieldhead, Amberley, Stroud, Gloucestershire GL5 5AG
Grants are made only within the county of Gloucestershire and mostly to registered charities.

Lord Leverhulme's Charitable Trust*
The Joint Secretary, The Barbinder Trust, Abacus House, Gutter Lane, London EC2V 8AH
*Priority is given to projects in Cheshire and to major national appeals by registered charities
only.*

The Manifold Charitable Trust
21 Dean's Yard, London SW1Y 3PA
*Particular interest in the preservation of historic buildings, but only for work carried out by
registered charities.*

Macdonald-Buchanan Charitable Trusts
The Secretaries, 1 Serjeant's Inn, London EC4Y 1JD
Preference is given to charities of which the appropriate trust has special knowledge.

Michael Marks Charitable Trust
W. H. Fisher & Co, Acre House, 69/76 Long Acre, London WC2E 9JW
Reference similar to Macdonald-Buchanan Charitable Trusts.

The Marsden Charitable Trust
11 Hall Close, Kibworth, Harcourt, Leicestershire LE8 0NP
Grants are made in April and November to registered charities only.

The Julian Melchett Trust*
The Secretary, 9 Albert Embankment, London SE1 7SN
*Projects should be of benefit to steel industry areas with priority to areas where the industry
is being run-down. Usually single grants are given to support capital or special projects.*

The Peter Minet Trust
The Secretary, 54 Knatchbull Road, London SE5 9QY
Interest in projects by registered charities related to objects of a unique or original nature.

The Monument Trust
The Administrator, 13 New Row, St Martin's Lane, London WC2N 4LF
Grants are made on a wide basis for schemes having national interest, such as the Wirksworth project. The Monument Historic Buildings Trust is a separate trust which buys, restores and sells buildings on its own account.

The Mount Trust*
The Administrator, Box TN1, Talbot House, Talbot Court, Gracechurch Street, London EC3V 0BS
Preference to charities of which the trust has particular knowledge, with a bias towards the south east and London. Preservation of historic buildings and the industrial heritage a special interest.

Nineveh Charitable Trust*
Little Nineveh, Benenden, Cranbrook, Kent TN17 4LG
Projects related to education in Scotland, of outstanding interest and involving individuals rather than institutions.

The John William Odell Charitable Fund Ltd.
Claude Baker & Partners, 22 Station Road, Watford SD1 1EP
Grants are made on a general, national basis for charitable purposes.

The Peacock Charitable Trust
86 Bushey Road, Rayner Park, London SW20 0JJ.
Help is given to charities of which the trustees have special knowledge.

The Pilgrim Trust
The Secretary, Fielden House, Little College Street, London SW1P 3SH
The trust specialises in aiding the preservation of the national heritage and in projects related to art and learning. Grants are made both locally and nationally.

Cecil Pilkington Charitable Trust
Coopers & Lybrand, Bridewell House, 6 Greyfriars Road, Reading, Berkshire RG1 1JG
Schemes should preferably be related to educational aspects of agriculture and forestry. Support is only given to registered charities in England and Wales.

Carew Pole Charitable Trust*
2 New Square, Lincoln's Inn, London WC2
The trust supports projects in or related to Cornwall.

The Michael and Audrey Sacher Charitable Trust
H. W. Fisher & Co, Acre House, 69/76 Long Acre, London WC2E 9JW

In the main, assistance is given to charities known personally to the trustees and principally to Jewish organisations. Its area of interest is wide.

The Scarfe Charitable Trust*
92a Hamilton Road, Felixstowe, Suffolk IP11 YAD.
Supports conservation projects in Suffolk.

Mrs Sunley's Second Charity Trust
The Secretary, The Cowdray Trust Ltd, Millbank Tower, Millbank, London SW1P 4QZ
Charitable projects covering a wide field.

The Second Mary Snow Trust
The Joint Secretary, The Barbinder Trust, Abacus House, Gutter Lane, Cheapside, London EC2V 8AH
Supports projects related to education and the countryside.

W. F. Southall Trust
Messrs Rutter and Rutter, Solicitors, 2 Brinfort, Shaftesbury, Dorset
The trust has an interest in projects related to the Society of Friends.

The St Levan Foundation*
21 Ennismore Gardens, London SW7
The charities assisted are only those with which the trustees have personal contact. Particular interest in Plymouth and West Cornwall.

The St Michael's Mount Foundation
The Manager, Manor Office, Marazion, Cornwall TR17 0HT
Principally concerned with the upkeep of the heritage.

The Janatha Stubbs Foundation
Messrs Deloitte, Haskins & Sells, Richmond House, 1 Rumford Place, Liverpool L3 9QS
Grants are made for general charitable purposes.

Swan Trust
The Secretary, The Cowdray Trust, 17th Floor, Millbank Tower, Millbank, London SW1P 4QZ
Grants are made for general charitable purposes.

The Westminster Foundation*
The Secretary, 53 Davies Street, London W1Y 1FH
The foundation has an emphasis on supporting projects related to youth, welfare, education and religion on a national basis but with special interests in Cheshire and the London area.

The above list is not comprehensive. It excludes any trusts that only made grants of three figures or less in the financial year 1981–2 and some, like the Morell Charitable Trust which helped with part of the Wirksworth project, having interests outside the specific field of historic buildings and only of relevance if the scheme touches on other aspects of a social or perhaps artistic nature. There are additional categories of grant-making trusts specialising in historic churches, the amenities of villages, towns and cities, town and country planning and urban studies. Information about these, and others, may be obtained from the *Directory of Grant-making Trusts*. The availability of grants depends not only on the suitability of the project but on the demands being made on the trust concerned at the time the application is made.

Appendix II
ARCHITECTS INVOLVED IN PROJECTS DESCRIBED

Barlaston, Barlaston Hall
Hunt Thompson Associates, 69 Parkway, London NW1 7PP

Belford, Belford Hall
Reavell & Cahill, Lloyds Bank Chambers, Alnwick, Northumberland NE66 1TG

Bradford-on-Avon, 5–8 Market Street
Vernon Gibbs Partnership, 15 Belmont, Bath BA1 5DZ

Bristol, 38–9 Market Street
Ferguson Mann, Royal Colonnade, 18 St George Street, Bristol BS1 5RH

Cromer, Gunton Hall
Robert Weighton, The Drying House, Malting No 6, South Road, Oundle, Peterborough PE8 4BU with Malcolm Leverington, 5 Church Street, Isleham, Ely, Cambridgeshire CB7 5RX

Derby, The Railway Cottages
Derek Latham and Associates, St Michael's Churchyard, Derby DE1 3SU

Edinburgh, Candlemaker Row and Glanville Place
Simpson and Brown, 179 Canongate, Edinburgh EH8 8BN

Edinburgh, 16–18 Calton Hill
Robert Hurd and Partners, 13 Manor Place, Edinburgh EH3 7DR

Essex, various schemes
The County Architect, County Hall, Chelmsford CM1 1LF

Kendal, Collin Croft
E. M. Bottomley of E. Donald Haigh, 29 Lowther Street, Kendal, Cumbria

Leiston, High Green
M. & S. Gooch, 11 Willow Lane, Norwich NR2 1EU, with the author

London, Southwark, Kirkcaldy's Testing Works
Duffy Eley Giffone Worthington (DEGW), 8–9 Bulstrode Place, Marylebone Lane, London W1N 5FW

London, Spitalfields, 5 and 7 Elder Street
Julian Harrap and Partners, 21a Stoke Newington Road, London N16 8XA

Market Harborough, Dingley Hall
Robert Weighton, The Drying House, Malting No 6, South Road, Oundle, Peterborough PE8 4BU

Sandy, Hazells Hall
Robert Weighton, The Drying House, Malting No 6, South Road, Oundle, Peterborough PE8 4BU with Malcolm Leverington, 5 Church Street, Isleham, Ely, Cambridgeshire CB7 5RX

Saxmundham, Angel Yard
Feilden & Mawson, Ferry Road, Norwich NR1 1SS, with the author

Woodbridge, 37–61 New Street
Feilden & Mawson, Ferry Road, Norwich NR1 1SS, with the author

BIBLIOGRAPHY

Since there is a considerable range of titles covering the various aspects of conservation the few below provide a very basic, and inevitably personal, reading list which could be multiplied several times over.

Binney, Marcus and Hanna, Max. *Preservation Pays: Tourism and the economic benefits of conserving historic buildings* (SAVE Britain's Heritage)
Binney, Marcus and Martin, Kit. *The Country House: to be or not to be* (SAVE Britain's Heritage)
Bunnel, Gene (Massachusetts Department of Community Affairs). *Built to Last* (The Preservation Press, 1977)
Cambridgeshire County Council. *A Guide to Historic Buildings Law* (Cambridgeshire County Council, 1984)
Esher, Lionel. *A Broken Wave: the rebuilding of England 1940–1980* (Pelican, 1983)
The Lord Montagu of Beaulieu. *Britain's Historic Buildings: A Policy for their Future Use* (British Tourist Authority)
Rock, David. *The Grassroot Developers: A handbook for town development trusts* (RIBA Conference Fund, 1980)
Royal Borough of Kensington & Chelsea. *Urban Conservation & Historic Buildings: A guide to the legislation* (Architectural Press, 1984)
Wirksworth Project/Civic Trust. *The Wirksworth Story: New Life for an Old Town* (Wirksworth Project in association with the Civic Trust, 1984)
Young, John. *The Country House in the 1980s* (George Allen & Unwin, 1981)

Miscellaneous
Architectural Heritage Fund. Annual Reports.
Civic Trust. *Environmental Directory.*
Charities Aid Foundation. *Directory of Grant-making Trusts.*
Directory of Social Change. *Fund raising* (eight booklets) (1984)

INDEX

Michell, Gordon, 97, 101, 102, 112, 113
Mitchell, Mary, 99, 104, 114
Monument Trust, 80, 87, 95
Morel charitable trust, 102
Mortgages, 60, 182
Moulton, Dr Alex, 14

National Council for Voluntary Organisations (NCVO), 161
National Heritage Memorial Fund, 86, 159
National Trust for Scotland (NTS), 8, 21, 22, 24, 29, 62; assitance to local societies and trusts, 30; Little Houses Improvement scheme, 21–30; Marquess of Bute survey, 22
National Westminster Bank, 13, 69, 111, 158
North East Civic Trust, 87
Northern Heritage Trust, 8, 87
Northern Ireland Tourist Board, 160
North West Civic Trust, 87

Pilgrim Trust, 16, 21, 49, 88, 148, 196
Planning permission, 177

Quantity surveyor, 46, 172

Repairs notice, 141
Repair process and philosophy, 75–8
Revolving fund, 7, 15–18, 22–51, 59–66, 105, 119, 140–4
Ripley, Golden Valley, 59, 60
Rothwell, Northamptonshire, 118, 120
Royal Institute of British Architects (RIBA), 7, 172, 173
Royal Institution of Chartered Surveyors (RICS), 75

SAVE Britain's Heritage, 8, 80–6
Saxmundham, Suffolk, Angel Yard, 36–43; alternative plans, 39, 40; cramped working conditions, 41; crinkle crankle wall, 41; delays, 42; effect on the town centre, 36;

exchange of properties, 39; formal opening, 42; grant, 40; local house prices, 36; market appeal, 42; parking or garage space, 42, 43; phasing, 39–41; publicity, 40, 42; range of accommodation, 41; residential density, 42; sales, 42; shop unit, 39; supervision, 40; tender prices, 39
Scotland, 21–30
Scottish burghal system, 22
Scottish Tourist Board, 62, 160
Seven Pillars of Wisdom Trust, 78
Solicitor, 172
Southwark, 67–70; commercial re-use of Kirkaldy's, 68; Industrial Buildings Preservation Trust, 68; Kirkaldy family, 67; Kirkaldy Testing Museum, 68; testing machine, 67, 68; Urban and Economic Developments Limited (URBED), 68–70
Spitalfields, 71–9; Christ Church, 71, 72; decline of, 71; Huguenot silk weavers, 71; reintroduction of residential use, 78, 79; 5 and 7 Elder Street, 72–9; finance, 78; first aid measures, 72; influence of the Elder Street scheme, 78–9; later projects, 78; locational advantages, 72; market assessment, 79; occupation by the Trust, 72; repair process and philosophy, 75–8; Spitalfields Trust, 71
Statutory requirements, 177
Statutory undertakers, 179
Strathclyde regional council, 29
Suffolk County Council, 31, 32, 35
Suffolk Coastal District Council, 7, 15, 18, 30–51; Agate, Grace, 50; Angel Yard, Saxmundham, 36–43; benefit of renovation to the community, 51; financial pressures, 50–1; Forton, Sidney, 50; Gordon, Victor, 30; Hansen, John, 30; High Green, Leiston, 43–51; New Street, Woodbridge,

31–6; policy for the use of the fund, 30, 31; purchasers, 50; revolving fund, 30
Technical assistance, 172, 173
Tourism, 108, 115
Tourist Boards, 159
Town schemes, 157

Urban and Economic Developments Limited (URBED), 68–70 *see also* Southwark

Value added tax (VAT), 18, 125

Wales Tourist Board, 160
West Wiltshire District Council, 12
Wirksworth, Derbyshire, 95–116; Abbey National Building Society, 105, 111, 114; aims of the Civic Trust, 96; Anthony Gell comprehensive school, 97, 101, 102, 113; Carnegie United Kingdom Trust, 111; chamber of trade, 97, 112; civic society, 100, 101, 116; conservation area, 104, 116; decline of, 95; Derbyshire Historic Buildings Trust, 105, 114; Development Commission, 107; English Tourist Board (ETB), 111; Europa Nostra medal, 113;

general improvement area, 104, 105; Hedges, Alan, 97–9; heritage centre, 108, 111; job creation, 107 115; key buildings, 105–7; landscape survey, 99, 100; limestone quarry, 95; Marsden charitable trust, 103; Monument trust, 95; Morel charitable trust, 102; National Westminster Bank, 111; National stone centre, 111; Schools' involvement, 101; shops, 108; tourism, 108; Town Council, 102, 103, 112; town scheme, 103; town survey and report, 97–9
Woodbridge, Suffolk, New Street, 31–6; blighting effect of planning proposals, 31; county and district council liaison, 31, 32; encouragement given to similar work, 35, 36; grant aid, 32; increase in market value, 36; phasing, 31, 33; policy for sales, 34; publicity, 34, 40; purchase of additional properties, 33; residential density, 35; tender negotiated, 34; tender procedure, 32, 33; travelling exhibition, 40; value to the street scene, 32
World of Property Housing Trust Scottish Housing Association, 29